RVing & Your Retirement Lifestyle:

A Cost Effective Way to
Live Your Dreams

Booklocker.com, Inc.
2009

RVing & Your Retirement Lifestyle:

A Cost Effective Way to
Live Your Dreams

Jeffrey Webber

TABLE OF CONTENTS

INTRODUCTION

You'll notice that the title of this book indicates that the RV lifestyle is a cost effective way to live your dreams. Do you find that difficult to believe? With the substantive information that follows, you will gain a perspective on how this is possible.

Consider for a moment that there will not be a need for expensive airplane tickets, which you know are outrageously high these days due to the cost of jet fuel. In addition there are no hotel room charges, no need for a rental car, and no need to eat out every day and night since you can prepare your meals in the comfort of your RV. Believe me when I tell you we've prepared some incredible gourmet meals in our coach.

Can you imagine the sensation of truly losing your sense of time? How would it feel to have to regularly check a calendar to see what the date is? That is basically how we live when we our traveling in our RV. This is a true sense of freedom. Our lifestyle is free and spontaneous.

For the last forty years we have been following our dreams in a recreational vehicle. And now, we have the additional advantage of being able to pursue our retirement interests.

As a retiree, it is crucial that you contemplate what you want from retirement. It is of the utmost importance that you have a retirement plan. Do you want to continue to grow and learn? Or, do you simply want to relax? Maybe you'd like to reinvent yourself and continue working part time. During our Third Age, (the first being childhood and the second family and career) we can experiment with new interests and ideas. We are living longer and healthier lives. The RV lifestyle will offer you the means to implement your plans. And, over the long term, you'll find that regardless of fluctuating fuel prices, you can do this economically. We do know this to be true because we are doing it right now.

To make this book work for you, it is imperative to find out if you can adjust your lifestyle to the RV way of life. Are there encumbrances that will prevent you from leaving your home? For example, are there family members that you must attend to? What about care and maintenance of your home? Do you have pets to provide for?

Can you afford to do this? Have you thought about a new concept called workcamping? We will discuss this and present information that will assist you in cost determinations.

In my first book, entitled *The New Professional Person's Retirement Lifestyle*, you are provided with a plethora of ideas for your retirement. The chapter on Volunteerism discusses a variety of ways you can help others around the country. One of the most important resources for RV volunteers is the National Park Service, where you can serve as a host in a National Park Campground (and be provided a free campsite at the same time). Or, how about Habitat for Humanity? Chapter after chapter suggests specific activities at various destinations that will readily compliment the RV lifestyle. You will, in effect, be able to travel with a purpose.

A most important consideration is that the RV lifestyle can be whatever you'd like it to be. You develop a style that fits your needs. In planning your RV retirement lifestyle, I recommend that you consider the Five R's:

- Reinvent yourself
- Rediscover yourself
- Rethink your goals
- Redefine yourself
- Revitalize your perspective

CHAPTER 1: WHAT DO I WANT FROM RETIREMENT? START WITH A PLAN!

If you are beginning your Third Age (there's that new terminology again), and you are considering the costly purchase of an RV, you really do need to set some goals for yourself.

It is important for you to take stock of yourself and formulate a course of action that you will definitely follow. You will need to engage in some thoughtful self-analysis to assist you in focusing on what you really want to do during retirement.

Here are some important considerations when developing that plan.

- Take a personal inventory. Consider your personal strengths and things that you would like to do better.

- Start simply and do not overburden yourself. Attempt to create a balance in your life between activities and recreation.

- Be creative! Remember, we are living longer, more healthy lives

- Remember the R words: reinvention; rediscovery; redefinition; revitalization; realization

When you've come up with a course of action, then we can begin to think about the RV lifestyle.

My wife and I have been RVers for forty years. We've always had the perspective that the RV lifestyle is a kind of tool. It can help you put together and implement plans and that you've devised.

Certainly, a mainstay of the RV lifestyle is the support it gives you if you have leisure activities in that all-important plan. I am reminded of Ernie Zelinski's book, *The Joy of Not Working*. He encourages you to consider leisure activities that turn you on now, new activities that you have considered doing, and activities that will get you physically fit. So, if part of your plan includes playing golf, biking, fishing, hiking, or swimming, your RV can obviously take you where the action is.

In my first book, *The New Professional Person's Retirement Lifestyle,* I discuss chapter after chapter of things to do during your retirement. If you incorporate ideas from the book into your retirement plan, your RV can become your real base of operations. For example, if you are interested in volunteerism, you can readily volunteer from the comfort of the rig, or, the rig can accommodate you while at a volunteer destination. The same scenario applies to working while camping, commonly called workamping. These topics will be discussed later chapters.

In essence, your recreational vehicle becomes a tool with which to implement your retirement plan. My wife and I pursue cultural interests, hobbies, we continue our education, and we invest, all in the comfort of our RV.

In 2006 we traveled across the country during the winter months in our Class A motorhome. Choosing from a variety of attractions from guidebooks and various websites, we chose to visit the Georgia O'Keefe Museum (one of the most famous art museums) in Santa Fe, New Mexico. We were able to locate a city campground with public transportation available right outside the gate. During our stay, we dined at various restaurants and enjoyed other cultural attractions. Additionally, we had all the comforts of home available in the RV including cable TV and wireless Internet. We enjoyed similar experiences in Las Cruces, New Mexico and Tucson, Arizona.

My wife and I love to bike. We own a tandem and we've biked in various locations around the country in an effort to explore the natural beauty of our country. So, when we reach a destination to bike, we do so directly from the campground from our home on wheels.

Again, all of these activities go toward achieving a goal that is part of our long-term plan for retirement.

I'll discuss more ways this can work in forthcoming chapters of this book.

CHAPTER 2: THE RV LIFESTYLE: COACHES & CAMPS

What do you think the term "RV lifestyle" really means? Well folks, the terminology is really simple to comprehend.

Your RV lifestyle is whatever you want it to be. If you have that all-important plan for retirement in hand, an RV can be a great tool to help implement that plan. When you think about it, your RV can actually assist in the planning of your retirement.

With all of the conveniences contained within an RV, even simple tasks such as going to the shopping mall, or the beach, or to most tourist attractions become more enjoyable.

We have found it most enjoyable to travel around with our living room, kitchen, and bathroom. When hiking or picnicking these facilities make the experience even more enjoyable. Certainly, van conversions, truck campers, and in general, small rigs work very well in these situations.

There are certain other conveniences that are specific to an RV. For example, you will not need to pack any suitcases. You will not need to catch an airplane, and, you eat in a restaurant only when you want to. If you find a location that you are particularly fond of, you may even be able to store your unit in a campground facility and perhaps have it moved on site when you arrive. Then when you leave, the RV is returned to the storage lot.

The RV lifestyle is very popular in part because of the freedom you have to stop whenever you choose to do or see whatever you'd like. The following is a sample of how various celebrities feel about the lifestyle:

- Jeff Daniels, actor: "I don't think you can call yourself a true American until you've been behind the wheel of an RV ... I love seeing parts of the country I wouldn't otherwise."
- Clarence Thomas, U.S. Supreme Court Justice: "Being an RVer helps me do my job better. The RV world gives me a chance to balance things out. It allows me a sense of freedom."
- Jeff Gordon, NASCAR driver, "My RV is the only place where I can find some peace and quiet."
- Bob Gibson, Hall of Fame major league pitcher: "I enjoy the RV world. I will have one until the day I die."
- Matthew McConaughey, actor: "There's nothing not to like about it. The freedom of being able to pull up, stop,

power up anywhere you want - beach or whatever. Set up and have your front yard different every single day."

- Jim Kaat, former major league baseball pitcher: "I've gone from being a major league pitcher to a major league RV owner. I'll travel roughly 5,000 miles in my RV this year. It's a great way to see America, and as relaxed a way to see the country as there can possibly be."

- Dean Karnazes, ultra marathon runner and best-selling author: "It's great for family bonding and eating healthy on the road, because you can prepare your own foods."

- Sue Henry, best-selling mystery writer: "You meet so many people in an RV. And they're so friendly. I couldn't do the research I do without one. In an RV, I can park and have everything I need."

- Davis Love, pro golfer: "I've got my bed, my pillows, my satellite card, my underwear and socks in the RV."

- Bode Miller, U.S. Olympic skier: "My team is sabotaging me by not letting me sleep in my motorhome."

Much of what determines your RV lifestyle is simply what you are planning on doing with the RV. You will need to ask yourself questions such as:

- How can an RV help me in pursuing my hobbies and interests?
- Where are you going to go?
- Will you be staying at a destination for a while, or, will you be moving around every few days?
- How long will you go? Many RVers travel extensively from perhaps six weeks to six months at a time before returning to home base.

  Snowbirds are usually RV people who reside in northern climates who escape to the south for the winter.

  Full-timers are campers who may have basically sold their possessions and made their RV their year round home. I'll talk more about this type of Rving in another chapter.
- How many people will be accompanying you? Do you have children or grandchildren that will come along? If this is the case, sleeping capacity will be in important issue for your consideration.

  The NADA (National Automobile Dealers Association) suggests that you spend a great deal of time evaluating your own personal situation. You really do want to make the right choice that takes into account your lifestyle and your wallet. You may be in a different market than a large family with a limited income.

To help you develop your own RV lifestyle, a discussion of some RV basics would be appropriate at this time.

Let's begin with a discussion of RV types. The two main types are motorized or towable. For a discussion on the cost of these RVs see Chapter 3.

TYPES OF RECREATIONAL VEHICLES
Motorized RVs

Normally, a motorhome would offer a variety of amenities including cooking facilities, refrigeration, a self-contained toilet, heating and or air conditioning, a portable water system, an electric system, sleeping facilities and a LP gas supply. So, what that really means is that they are self-contained. You drive it and live in it.

Many motorhome owners prefer to tow a car behind them. I tow a Honda CRV behind my coach because it fuel efficient, tracks well (follows the coach with ease), and is one of the few small SUVs that can be "flat towed" (towed behind the motorhome on all four wheels). There is no need to hook up a car trailer. If you do not care to tow a vehicle then you will have to unhook the RV and drive it out and about, which can be challenging if you have a large rig.

Before I discuss the basic motorhome types, it is relevant here to present to you some information on diesel engine power, since diesel power is readily available on all the classes and the information below clearly relates to cost effectiveness.

Certainly, diesel varieties can cost substantially more. Some advantages of diesel engine power follow:

- Durability – if you plan to keep your RV for many years and drive lots of miles, diesel is the obvious choice.

- Economy – Diesels do get better mileage than gasoline engines under the same weight and road conditions. However, since you pay more for a diesel the cost of the coach should be amortized by the fuel mileage.

- Resale Value - Generally, a diesel coach does hold its value better than a gas unit.

Some disadvantages of diesel power include:

- Cost – The cost of a diesel engine is several times that of a gasoline engine.

- Noise – Since diesel engines produce higher levels of noise than gas engines, the difference may be difficult for some to tolerate.

- Maintenance – The cost of maintenance is higher for diesel engines and, if you neglect that maintenance, it can be very expensive.

A discussion about the three basic motorhome types follows:

CLASS A MOTORHOMES

Class A coaches are built on a specially constructed chassis. They can range in length from twenty-five to forty-five feet.

Many Class A coaches feature slideouts. That simply means that you push a button and a portion of the living area slides out, allowing you substantially more living area. Actually, the difference can be quite dramatic depending on the size of the coach.

Normally, the more that you spend on the cost of the coach, the more you can expect in terms of amenities. Examples of these goodies include electric awnings, flat screen TVs, heated ceramic tile floors, dishwashers, trash compactors, and even a fireplace.

And then there are the more luxurious motorcoaches that can cost upwards of one million dollars. They are constructed on a special bus type chassis and can be built with high-end components.

Major advantages of the Class A coach include ease of handling. I have always felt that driving my motorhome is comparable to driving a luxury automobile in terms of visibility and handling.

CLASS B AND B+ MOTORHOMES

Most of these coaches are built on a van chassis with an elevated roof so you can stand up inside. Lengths range from seventeen to twenty-one feet. Accommodations in these RVs are quite compact. Think of it in terms of attempting to fit the same amenities that are in a Class A into a Class B. Because of this lack of space, these rigs may not be well suited for long-term trips or extended living. I guess it all depends on how well you get along with your travel partner.

Major advantages of these coaches are their maneuverability and fuel economy. You may be able to easily get along without having to tow another vehicle. You will find it easy to get around town to grocery shop and park in tight spaces. An important consideration is that these RVs can be quite costly. In fact, you may be able to purchase a larger Class C motorhome for the same price.

A relatively new RV design is the Class B+ coach. Basically, they are a step up in size from a Class B, but still smaller than a Class C. Many Class B+ coaches are available with one, two, or three slideouts.

CLASS C MINI-MOTORHOMES

These motorhomes are built on a heavy-duty van type chassis and include both a driver and passenger door. They are available with either gas or diesel engines

Class C coaches often attract buyers on a budget. Typical buyers include Rvers who are downsizing from a Class A, or, larger families. Many of these rigs often come with cab-over beds to increase the overall sleeping capacity. Or, if you prefer, many manufacturers offer the option of an entertainment center in lieu of the overhead bed. Additionally, they can be built with many of the same amenities that are featured in the larger RVs. The average length of a Class C can range from twenty-one feet to thirty-two feet.

TRUCK CAMPERS

The least expensive of the motorized category, truck campers can be built in consideration of any level of convenience. So, you can add a hard-sided camper shell to your pick-up truck, which will provide you with a protected environment to sleep as well as cargo space to carry stuff.

You also have the option of buying a more luxurious truck camper, which can be self-contained with all the amenities that you'd need. It is important to note here interior space in these campers is the most modest in the industry.

Truck campers have long been the favorite of outdoor types because of their ability to go just about anywhere,

Towable Recreational Vehicles

As the name implies, a towable RV is one that is towed behind another RV. These are commonly referred to trailers. Most often the tow vehicle (towing the towable) is a pickup truck, SUV, van, or even another small, motorized RV that is equipped with a tow package.

Types of trailers include the following:

FIFTH WHEEL TRAILERS

These trailers are most easily recognizable by the raised front section. This part of the trailer hooks up to a fifth-wheel hitch that sits inside of the truck. Fifth-wheel trailer lengths range from twenty-one to forty feet. The interiors are usually very roomy. They handle better than conventional trailers particularly when it comes to cornering. During the years I owned one of these rigs, there were few drivability situations that I was unable to handle.

The overall length of the trailer and its tow vehicle is less than a travel trailer because the front section of the fifth-wheel sits in the bed of the truck.

One distinct advantage of a fifth-wheel trailer is its increased support and stability when towing. You do not have to be concerned about fishtailing and wind gusts when traveling. Additionally, the amenities in these rigs can be quite luxurious, and, slideouts are very common.

Many full-timers choose 5th wheels as their home on wheels because of previously mentioned advantages as well as a lot of roominess.

TRAVEL TRAILERS

Travel trailers come in a large variety of floorplans and lengths. They can range in length from thirteen feet to around thirty-five feet. As with most other RVs, they have their own heating, air-conditioning, and electrical systems. These trailers can be purchased very economically, if desired. They are available in a variety of trim levels.

Tow vehicles can include a properly equipped full-size car, SUV, or pick-up truck. You may have to equip your vehicle with a load equalizing hitch and other devices to make the ride more comfortable.

CAMPING TRAILERS

These trailers are also known as pop-ups. They are easily identifiable by their collapsible walls made of canvas of fiberglass. Newer models provide many of the amenities found in other RVs including sinks, stoves, and refrigerators. You can even get one with a toilet and shower. Certainly a major advantage of these units is fuel economy because they are low profile and lightweight. They do allow for a feeling of open-air tent camping. Sleeping accommodations can keeps as many as eight people comfortable.

Camping trailers are probably the easiest RV to tow and maneuver. So, if you think you'll prefer to stay in remote areas that are mainly state and national parks with limited facilities, for shorter periods of time, this may be your logical choice. And, you will genuinely feel the spirit of the outdoors surrounding you.

During the past forty years, my wife and I have had every type of RV. We have attempted to own an RV that best supports our lifestyle at the time. So, in early years when we both worked lots of hours and money was tight, the clear choice was a small travel trailer. That choice allowed us to drive an economical vehicle on a daily basis. If we did not have the time to camp, we did not feel so bad about leaving the trailer in the driveway because the initial outlay was minimal.

As our family expanded, and we had more time to travel, we moved up to a large fifth-wheel trailer. As fifth wheels are relatively easy to maneuver, we traveled to lots of state and National Parks and ultimately used the trailer as a winter abode in a campground near ski areas.

When the kids began to leave home, we switched to a Class C motorhome because we began to do a lot more traveling during the summer months. As we were both educators, an abundant amount of time was available.

When retirement came on the scene, we switched to a Class A motorhome because we began to spend a considerable amount of time on the road and added space was desired.

Toy Haulers: The Newest Sensation

Seeing that a goal of this book is to encourage you to pursue your hobbies and interests, your best choice for an RV may be a toy hauler.

In case you are not familiar with the term, a toy hauler can be a motorhome, 5th wheel trailer, or travel trailer. This RV is designed to allow RVers to bring along their "toys." Those include ATVs, motorcycles, and or snowmobiles. Normally, a toy hauler is divided into two parts: a living area in the front and a garage type storage area in the rear.

A major impact on your decision to purchase a toy hauler depends on what you'd like to do on the open road. If you enjoy the open air and the adventurous lifestyle that would necessitate a "toy." then this choice would be a good option for you. You'd really have to decide how much use you expect to get out of the hauler part of the RV and if you can indeed live within the smaller living area.

Making the Right Choice

Now that you have some background on the various types of RVs available, there are some additional considerations to ponder that will assist you in selecting the right RV for your situation. For information on cost considerations see Chapter 3, Costs & Cost Saving Strategies.

WHO IS GOING CAMPING?

It is always a good idea to put in perspective who is going to be camping in the RV. Will it be just the two of you, or, will your three grandchildren be accompanying you on your trips? If they do go with you, how often will that be? We've found that a realistic cost effective measure these days, given the high cost of fuel and the high cost of RVs, is to keep that handy dandy tent in the RV in case of additional house guests. This allows us to have the rig that we really want. In our case, we really do prefer a small unit.

If you do decide to make that headcount a basis for the decision, be certain that you check a variety of floorplans. Obviously you will need room for everybody to sleep. But you may want to put some thought into room to move about so that travelers can have their space.

WHERE ARE YOU HEADED?

Your choice of RV can be greatly influenced by the kind of camping you expect to do. This is the point in the selection process where it is good to consider your retirement goals along with hobbies and interests. For example, if you like to play golf, tennis, and enjoy swimming, then perhaps you'll be interested in resort campgrounds. Most resort campgrounds can accommodate any size rig.

On the other hand, if you prefer more remote state and National Parks, the size of your RV becomes an important consideration. These parks may have specific size restrictions, which may preclude a larger rig.

As part of the aforementioned discussion, you should note that the shorter the overall length of your RV, the easier it is to manipulate. That includes parking, backing up, or changing lanes.

WHAT DO I NEED TO HAVE ONBOARD?

If you absolutely have to have a huge kitchen, along with a washer and dryer, and a large flat screen television, then you may not be able to get that camping trailer or small travel trailer.

GAS OR DIESEL MOTORHOME

As of this writing, the cost of gasoline and diesel fuel is in flux. Additionally, the cost of the diesel coach is dramatically more. This cost may be worth it if you decide to go for a larger motorhome as a rear-mounted diesel will provide additional power.

Try the RV Lifestyle!

If you've never experienced the RV lifestyle for a period of time, it is critical that you do a "test drive" of sorts. That is, rent an RV and go out for a few weeks.

RV rentals are a great way to travel. You can vacation, visit new places, and at the same time, figure out what kind of RV best suits you.

Before you rent you will want to consider choices of destinations, and exactly how much time you have available. Be certain that you plan well enough in advance as rental agencies to get quite busy during periods of warm weather.

You will also want to think about who is going on the trip and the interests of everyone. That may affect the size of the rig that you rent.

If you do decide to rent, be sure to read all the details of the rental agreement so you will know about any additional charges, insurance issues, and charges per mile. Do not be fearful of shopping around. Fees are very competitive. You may be able to rent from a local agency, or, you can travel to pick up the rig to a location farther away. The advantage of traveling to rent is that you may be interested in exploring an area a distance away, and it may be easier to travel to that location and rent.

If you are not sure as to which RV is for you, feel free to rent one of each. All of the various are available for you. That will provide you with some decision-making assistance. In addition, I suggest that you rent a rig for as long as possible in effort to gain a great deal of personal experience with the day-to-day routines. You will then have several opportunities to drive it, park it, dump the holding tanks, hooking and unhooking, and cook in the RV.

At the time of this writing, the average price of a Class C motorhome rental is about $1000 per week. Those coaches will usually sleep up to seven people. The cost of renting a luxury rig is ninety to two hundred dollars per day. More modest travel trailers were costing twenty-eight to eighty-five dollars per day. Many rental agencies offer packages that include linens and pots and pans so you do not have to worry about packing all of that.

Be certain to pay special attention to the tutorial you receive before you drive off from the agency. You will learn about every system in the RV. Take notes if you have to in order to avoid any confusion while on the road. Take it from me; after you've camped a couple of nights, you will become very familiar with routine operations.

The following rental agency websites are very helpful:

- Cruiseamerica (*cruiseamerica.com*) – the largest in the country
- Elmonte (*elmonterv.com)*
- Moturis (*moturis.com*)

CAMPGROUNDS

Most campgrounds fall into two basic categories: overnight and destination.

When we travel for longer time periods on Interstates, we typically look for those campgrounds that are that have easy on and off access. The intrinsic value of these campgrounds is convenience and not necessarily beauty. So, if they have cable tv and wi-fi access I am satisfied. Sometimes, however, if you have your handy campground guide handy, you may be able to locate a state park or private campground close by, so you do not have to listen to the sounds of the highway. And, if you are really lucky, you may come across a campground in that offers level, pull-through sites where little effort is required to set up camp.

Before we get into a discussion of campgrounds, here are some thoughts connecting your RV to campground utilities.

Joe and Vicki Kieva, who write a column for the Good Sam Club, suggest the following procedures to make the process easier:

- Before hooking up check the polarity and voltage on the electrical connection, clean up the water faucet, and clear any debris from the area.

- Turn off the breaker switch when plugging to prevent any possibility of a shock.

- Attach a water pressure regulator to the faucet followed by your water hose and then run some water to remove air from the hose.

- Hooking up the sewer hose is last. Make certain the connections are tight. They suggest you wear inexpensive disposable gloves when doing this.

- When you are all hooked up, you can open the grey water valve. The black water valve, however, should remain closed. The more liquid store in the black water tank, the better the flushing action when you do dump. After you've dumped the black water tank, flush two gallons of fresh water into the toilet to prevent any solidifying action.

DESTINATION CAMPGROUNDS – Here is where you will most likely spend a fair amount of time. If you are pursuing your interests and hobbies that are part of your retirement plan, these facilities are very convenient. Considerations such as a convenience store, laundry room, and pool may be of importance to you. RV resorts may be of interest. You may even find a golf course, tennis courts, and a marina attached to the campground.

IMPROVED CAMPGROUNDS - Most often these camps will offer gravel or paved campsites with electric and water hookups. Although a sewer hookup may not be available, a dump station would certainly be there. Usually, these campgrounds are commercially owned and may be franchised. An example of this is Kampgrounds of America (*koa.com*), which offers a free annually updated directory. There are more that 450 KOA franchises in the United States and Canada. Incidentally, KOA is an example of a franchise that offers convenient overnight locations off the Interstate. This is especially significant if you've been traveling all day and need a place to stop right off of the exit. My experience has been that you can count on these facilities to be there when you need them, especially when traveling during the winter months when the temperatures are substantially below normal.

Most improved RV parks can accommodate today's RVs. They are fully paved, level, free from low tree branches, and generally offer all the amenities you'd need, including wireless Internet.

RV RESORTS – These parks offer the same facilities as improved RV parks, but may include access to recreational amenities such as a golf course, tennis courts, or a marina. These resort most usually are found in a luxurious setting and may be associated with an adjacent resort hotel or casino. Guests can be entitled to the same privileges as guests of the hotel.

MEMBERSHIP CAMPGROUNDS – For some part-time Rvers, a membership campground represents a resort with many amenities to use as a less expensive ongoing vacation spot. An advantage of this approach is that there may be a reciprocal arrangement in place with similar resorts elsewhere in the country. Though you cannot stay there full-time you can elect, for additional money, to rent for months at a time.

Thousand Trails (*1000trails.com*), is one of the largest chains with at least fifty participating campgrounds. The initial buy-in is around $3000. You then have a number of free nights per year available to you. If you exceed that number, you must pay a small amount per night.

OVERNIGHT PARKING – Parking of RVs is permitted in some rest areas off of Interstates. Restaurants, truck stops, and chain stores such as Wal-Mart, may also allow self-contained RVs to stay overnight. For further information on free camping or "boondocking" see Chapter 3 in this book on Cost Saving Strategies.

SNOWBIRDS

Typically, Snowbirds keeps their home base. When the weather turns colder they would depart for warmer climates. So a recreational vehicle works out perfectly for this purpose. Your RV becomes your second home. Frequently, Snowbirds do make the transition to fulltimers because they do indeed enjoy the RV lifestyle and cannot get enough of it. For more information on fulltiming, see the Chapter in this book on fulltiming.

As snowbirds, we try to plan our longer trips to warmer destinations so that they are slow and relaxed. There is no rush. If the destination route is planned carefully, it can be inviting with interesting stops along the way.

Among the most popular destinations for Snowbirds are Florida, Texas, Arizona, California, and New Mexico.

In Florida, RV people head for most of the central and southern parts of the state. My wife and I do have a preference for the Florida Panhandle area that includes Destin and Panama City. Although the temperature is a bit cooler in the winter, it is less crowded and the waterfront camping is simply beautiful.

In Texas most people head for the Rio Grande Valley, while in Arizona, it is the Phoenix, Scottsdale, and Mesa Area. In California, the popular areas are Imperial, Riverside, and San Diego Counties.

Most Snowbirds seem to congregate in RV parks that cater to the fifty-five and older crowd as that is where a variety of activities are featured. Those activities include golf, tennis, swimming and bicycling, as well as a variety of evening events.

An increasingly popular practice these days is campsite ownership. A strong argument for this is that you never have to worry about find an available space in you favorite campground and, you can stay as long as you desire. For many fulltimers who have given up their homes, owning two campsites (north and south) is the clear choice. A major advantage of dual site ownership is not having to worry about one's home while away. And, when you add up the monetary savings on taxes, utilities, and maintenance, the prospects of site ownership become even more interesting. Of course, you can certainly rent a site on a long-term basis with the same results. In fact many Rvers buy a Park Model trailer and leave it on the site(s) year round.

Many Rvers have found that this snowbird routine encourages the development of a network of friends that they look forward to being with year after year.

CHAPTER 3: COSTS & COST SAVING STRATEGIES

If you've developed that all-important plan for retirement, it is safe to presume considerable thought has gone into the cost of implementing your lifestyle. As previously indicated, your RV is a costly tool in the creation of this lifestyle. So, it is crucial that you plan ahead to deal with the costs involved.

As you read about the various types of RVs available, you will see that prices can range anywhere from $4000 to over a million dollars. You may find yourself participating in a sort of ritualistic discussion of "what you like and what you can afford." If you are on a strict retirement budget, the former may win out.

Buying a Used RV

A major consideration will be whether to purchase a used rig. If you are thinking about buying "pre-owned," as the dealers like to say, then you may want to consider your potential for performing repairs; whether they be simple or more complex. You will also want to think about the history of the RV. That is, who used it, for how long, and were the previous owners faithful to regular maintenance. You'll also want to think about a manufacturer's warranty or obtaining an extended warranty.

Depending on the age and mileage of the unit, a warranty may be available. Additionally, when you search for a used rig, be sure to check out RV Trader (*rvtraderonline.com*) and Craigslist (*craigslist.org*) for bargains. I've had very good luck on both of these sites. There usually a variety of pictures posted for listing on these websites. You can check postings on eBay (*ebay.com*) as well, but the difficulty is in the examination of the unit before you purchase. If you are lucky, you may be able to locate an RV that is close enough for you to examine before the actual purchase.

If you area able to find an RV that interests you, be sure to look up the book value on the NADA site (*nadaguides.com*) to see if the price is reasonable. In addition, you can readily research specification information at the site. That is, you can ascertain important information relating to vehicle weights and capacities along with standard equipment and options. I cannot tell you how many times over the last forty-two years these efforts have saved my substantial amounts of money. Take the time to do the homework.

Should I Buy an Extended Warranty?

Then there is the matter of whether to purchase an extended warranty on your new or used rig.

I recently read an article in Highways, the journal of the Good Sam Club, about a gentleman who purchased a five-year old Class A Motorhome. Six months after the purchase the refrigerator needed to be replaced. The total cost of the replacement was $3600. That is a staggering amount of money to lay out for repair. When I bought my most current new RV, I did purchase an extended warranty that covered just about everything. My monthly payments were about one hundred dollars per month for twelve months. When you think about replacing big-ticket items in your RV such as slide-outs and leveling jacks, those payments seem minimal.

Be certain that you read and understand the terms of an agreement before writing a check. Also, it is important that the agreement covers big-ticket items such as those mentioned in the previous paragraph. You will also want to check where repairs can be completed. That is, do you have to travel a long distance to get the work done, or, can you arrange to have repairs done locally? In my case, I was able to take the coach to my local facility, and the warranty provider reimbursed me directly for the cost of the repairs.

Can I Afford This Thing?

Similar in nature to most major expenditures in life, you will have to put a great deal of thought into how much you can afford to put down, if you are going make monthly payments. If you have the capability to pay for the RV with cash, think about how much that cash is going to cost you:

- How much will the interest be on the loan?
- How much investment income will you lose from the money you put down?

If you are going to finance, be certain to obtain quotes from several finance companies. At the time of this writing, the downturn in the economy has led to some very attractive rates in an effort to stimulate sales. Be leery about zero percent financing as that can often lead to less of a discount on the actual RV. You will also want to be able to pay off the balance on your loan in the event of a windfall. In actuality, manufacturers frequently offer terrific financing incentives to promote sales.

Another major consideration these days, when figuring costs, is the fluctuating price of fuel. As I write this, the cost of gasoline is averaging around two dollars a gallon. Three months previously, the national average was four dollars per gallon. The cost of diesel fuel is currently significantly higher than the cost of gas. If you add the higher price of a diesel coach together with the fuel, the total can be staggering. If you living on a limited budget, fuel economy and RV costs may be important to you regardless of whether you purchase a gas or diesel coach.

If you are interested in towing a large travel trailer or fifth wheel trailer, you may need to use the tow vehicle on a daily basis when you are not camping. The cost of fuel for a heavy- duty vehicle may be prohibitive to your cash flow. Many RVers who travel with a motorized coach do tow a small vehicle that is used for campground excursions and daily usage at home. Fuel consumption thereby becomes a bit more manageable.

In consideration of this discussion, it is imperative that you try to plan ahead and consider the expected use of your RV now and in the future. This will give you some perspective on whether you will be able to afford to do this.

It is important to note that even with these costs, I have found that the RV lifestyle is considerably less expensive over the long haul in comparison to regular vacations. Of course, you do have to consider the initial outlay for the RV.

It is relatively simple to plan the costs of any RV trip if you

1. know the price range of fuel

2. can estimate campground fees and expenses for food

3. add some additional funds for entertainment.

General Cost Comparisons of Various Vacations

At the time of this writing, airfares are up fifteen to twenty percent due to the high price of fuel. That has lead to increases in hotels, meals dined out, and entertainment. The prospect of Rving becomes more of an affordable option even with the escalating gas prices.

Then, of course, there is the matter of the RV lifestyle. If you are an RVer, it is a lifestyle that is hard to shake no matter how high gas prices get. As you know by now, many retirees use their rigs year round and it is a great source of family recreation. In a recent survey by the Recreational Vehicle Industry Association, ninety three percent of RV owners said they expect to use their RVs more than ever, even with the rise in fuel prices.

PFK Consulting, a leading tourism research firm, came up with the conclusion that a family of four can spend up to seventy-four percent less when vacationing by RV. Big savings were incurred over travel by car or plane with hotel accommodations or rental properties. Even the most expensive RV trip can be one-third the cost of a cruise excursion and one-fifth the cost of an all-inclusive package getaway.

Here are some figures to accompany the discussion:

- When vacationing in a motorhome, the family would average $2996 for a fourteen day vacation as compared with $4222 when using a car and staying in hotels, $9053 when taking a cruise, and $5742 when flying, renting a car, and staying in hotels.

- When vacationing in a light-duty truck or SUV towing a trailer, the cost of that fourteen-day vacation would be $2837

- When vacationing in a folding camping trailer, the fourteen-day vacation would cost $2317.

- An all-inclusive vacation package for the same family and time period averages out at $9285.

Cost Saving Strategies

The authors of the previous study have come up with a list of some common sense tips to keep RVing affordable in light of higher fuel prices.

- <u>Camp closer to home</u>. Our forty years of camping experience has lead to a wonderful nucleus of campgrounds in the Northeast that we enjoy visiting.

- <u>Think about staying in one place for a longer period of time</u>. Many campgrounds offer substantial discounts for longer stays. When we camped last year in the desert of Arizona, the daily fee at that Casino camp was $43. After our month long stay, the fee was reduced to $32.

- <u>Cook your favorite meals in your RV to help avoid the high costs of eating out.</u> If you do dine out, look for specials in the form of coupons and early bird specials. Those deals are usually advertised in local newspapers. Sometimes it can be more cost effective to dine out for a late breakfast, lunch, or even a lunch buffet.

- Consolidate your short trips into a longer trip. Or, you can walk or take the bike (as we do) from the campsite, or, take public transportation.

- Pack lighter in an effort to keep the weight of the RV to a minimum.

- If you can, travel at night during the hot weather. That technique will reduce air conditioning requirements.

The website *rvbasics.com* has devised a list of frugal tips to make the RV lifestyle even more cost effective.

- Buy a frugal RV. Do you really need to buy that big luxury RV? You can have just as much fun in a good quality less expensive new or used rig.

- Look for low cost RV sites in city, state, or federal camping areas.

- Camp for free. There are many places where you can park overnight and even many days for free. Those locations include Wal-Marts, Bureau of Land Management lands, and Casinos. Always be certain that you've obtained appropriate permission to park in the parking lot of a commercial establishment.

- If you can, do your own RV maintenance. Good resources for you to check include websites and a variety of books that explain how to perform much of the care required.

- Do not buy all of your groceries at supermarkets. You may be able to get better buys at thrift bakeries, discount stores, dollar stores, flea markets, and roadside veggie stands.

Indeed, we've saved a great deal of money over the years at the Dollar Store and Target. You'll find a variety of low priced staples and sundries at both retail locations.

- Travel during the off-season for pre and post season discounts. Campgrounds and RV parks, theme parks, and other attractions routinely offer lower prices during the off-season.

In a recent article *cnnmoney.com* suggested RV appropriate ways to stop wasting gas. In essence, I've tried them all and the results clearly lead to a substantial savings that you can take to the bank. RVs are clearly not the most fuel-efficient vehicles and the following suggestions are definitely cost effective.

1. Don't race away from green lights. The more you press down on the gas pedal, the more gas you'll pump into the engine.

2. Don't race up to a red light. Lay off the gas if you see a red light ahead. Coasting gives your engine a chance to rest and will your brake pad life may be extended as well.

3. Don't confuse the highway with a speedway. In tests, Consumer Reports concludes that reducing your highway speed by ten miles per hour increases fuel economy by three to five miles per hour. By reducing my highway speed from sixty-five to fifty-seven I realize a fuel economy improvement in my Class A motorhome that increases from six to eleven mpg.

4. Don't let your vehicle idle. Idling burns about a half-mile worth of gas every minute, according to the California Energy Commission. That is why hybrid cars shut down their gasoline engines whenever they stop.

More Suggestions For Reducing Campground Fees

It is always good to remember that whenever you can reduce your expenses on the road, you'll need less income. Living the RV lifestyle can be less expensive in many respects because there are certain expenses that you can control.

Certainly, on any given night you will save money if you do not have to pay a campground fee. Indeed, those savings add up over a period of time. We've been to many private camps that charge up to fifty dollars per night. On the other hand, we've stayed at state parks that charge ten to twenty dollars per night with no hook-ups.

If you are working (or volunteering) at a campground you may receive a campsite free of charge. Sometimes, camping for free may be your remuneration for working.

Dry Camping

If your rig is self-contained, you can save substantial money by dry camping. That is, camping without hook-ups. Most commonly, these RV sites are found in a city, state, or federal campground. These parks usually charge a fee, but that fee is usually quite reasonable. For more information see Chapter 4 (Boondocking).

Additional Suggestions

Sightseeing

During all the years we've been Rving around this beautiful country of ours, sightseeing has been a priority. We do like to like to maintain this cost effective lifestyle in any way possible.

When arriving in a new area it is a good idea to check the local newspaper for attractions and coupons for those attractions. Frequently, the cost of admission to a particular location may be less expensive on some days. You will also want to check in at the local visitor center or chamber to see about the availability of those discount coupons.

If you belong (and there is no reason why you should not) to The Good Sam Club, AARP, AAA, FMCA or any other travel club additional discounts may be available.

If you enjoy our National Parks and Federal Recreational Lands as much as we do, and you are over the age of sixty-two, why not obtain an America the Beautiful (formerly Golden Age Passport) lifetime pass. The cost is only ten dollars and you will be provided with access and use of any Federal site that charges and entrance fee. Further, if you volunteer at a National Park or Federal recreation site that charges a fee, and you've accumulated five hundred hours of service, you may be eligible for a free volunteer pass.

More tips on saving energy

Do not forget the simple things when driving your RV.

For example, keep your tires properly inflated. Not only will you be safer, but also, you will increase your gas mileage.

I always use the cruise control on my motorcoach. You can increase mileage by as much as fifteen percent.

Another useful energy saving tip when parking your RV at the campsite is this: take into account the position of the sun. In this way, you can take advantage of passive solar heating, especially when the temperatures begin to cool down. In addition, when the temperatures are hot, take full advantage of any shade potential. Don't forget to open your awning. You will fully realize the gains here when you are dry camping.

We have found over the years, that it is definitely more economical to travel on the lightweight side. That is, lose some pounds. If you go through your storage closets and compartments and find items that have been unused for a period of time, take them out. Additionally, you do not necessarily need to travel with your water tanks completely full, unless you are dry camping and water is unavailable.

If you are driving a motorcoach and you need to tow a "dinghy" behind your vehicle, try to choose the lightest, smallest car to minimize your extra fuel consumption. Believe me when I tell you, I've been through the mill with tow vehicles, and size does indeed realize substantial dollar savings.

Budgeting

Much of the preceding discussion has specific budget implications. If you are retired and would like to spend a great deal of time on the road in your RV, budget considerations may be very important to you. Once you've gotten over the "what to buy for an RV" hump, and affordability issues have been decided, a specific budgeting plan may be helpful to you.

I've found that input from campers on budgeting can be very helpful in the planning process.

When you've gathered relevant monetary information it is useful to be able to format into a readable table. Our longtime friends and RVers Ed and Julie Engel from North Carolina have been retired for a few years. They travel in their Class C Motorhome an average of about a dozen trips per year within a well-planned budget. They utilize the two worksheets below to help them track and adjust expenses. As the sheets were created in Microsoft Excel, you can certainly modify the criteria to meet your own needs. The following accompanying comments are offered as an addendum to their approach:

- The Trip Planning sheet is used to calculate anticipated expenses for an RV trip that are beyond expenses that would be incurred if they stayed at home. For example, groceries are not included as an expense

- Whenever possible Ed and Julie purchase in bulk from a wholesale club. Of course, this approach depends your storage capabilities.

- Fixed RV costs (RV insurance, RV property tax, and RV storage) are indicated in the budget sheet since they are a constant.

- Laundry costs are more due to the prices at Laundromats.

- While away from home, savings can be incurred with the adjustment of heating and air-conditioning systems. (We've found over the long haul substantial savings can be realized, particularly during lengthy trips).

RV Budget Criteria

Summary:

Monthly	
Income:	0.00
Expenditures:	0.00
Balance:	0.00

Annual	
Income:	0.00
Expenditures:	0.00
Balance:	0.00

Income			Expenditures	
SS			CLHO/W	
SS			Raintree	
Pension			Electricity	
NC Pension			Gas	
Cref			Telephone	
			Cell phone	
			Time Warner Cable	
			Auto Insurance	
			Homeowner Insurance	
			Car operations	
			Groceries	
			Restaurants	
			Gifts	
			Supplemental Insurance	
			Rx Plan	
			Dental	
			Home Equity Loan (RV)	
			Haircuts	
			Pest Control	
			Clothing	
			RV Storage	

			RV Insurance	
			RV Tax	
			Estimate of income tax	
			Property Tax	
			Auto Tax	
			RV Camping Costs 1/	
			Emergencies	
			Gardening	

1/ RV Camping costs based on:		9	Short trips
		3	Long trips
Short trip =	3	Nights
Long trip =	30	Nights

RV Trip Cost Estimator

Gasoline/gall	$4.0
RV Mileage	8.5
Campgrounds	$25

Short trips:		Long trips:	
Nights away	3	Nights away	30
Days driving	2	Days driving	10
Avg miles/day	250	Avg miles/day	300
Campground cost	$75	Campground cost	$750
Gasoline cost	$235.29	Gasoline cost	$1,411.76
Total for 1 trip:	$310.29	Total for 1 trip:	$2,161.76
Annual number of trips:	9	Annual number of trips:	3
Annual cost short trips:	$2,792	Annual cost long trips:	$6,485.29
Monthly cost:	$232.72	Monthly cost:	$540

MONTHLY TOTAL BOTH SHORT AND LONG	$773

Please note: Obviously your expenses would vary from these figures given the volatility of fuel costs and specific mileage you experience. Additionally, Ed and Julie prefer to stay in state parks that are traditionally less expensive than private parks.

You'll also notice that the daily cost of the longer-term trips are less simply because they stay put for a longer time period.

CHAPTER 4: BOONDOCKING: A GREAT WAY TO SAVE MONEY & ENJOY NATURE

Boondocking is the term that denotes camping without electric and water hookups, water faucets, sewer hookups, and phone or cable TV connections. In addition, there are no campground fees. This usually means wilderness or primitive camping out in the "boondocks." It is important to note that typically, boondocking RVers are people who have self-contained Rvs.

There are as many reasons to boondock as people to ask why they boondock! Here are some common reasons:

- Experience the fun and freedom to go where you want. Imagine being surrounded by natural beauty, with little or no neighbors. There is nothing more comforting than awakening in the morning with the sound of a stream and a distant view of a spectacular mountain range.

- We want to save money! Often times the primary reason for boondocking may be to experience natural beauty. A second primary reason can be to save money. Certainly, this is valid for retirees living on fixed incomes.

And, it further substantiates how cost effective RVing can be.

- Another thought that comes to mind in regards to saving money is that boondocking can help to equalize RVing expenses. In particular, it may make it easier for you to deal with the high cost of fuel. Basically, the nights that you boondock can offset the nights that you pay high private campground fees.

- Boondocking is convenient! Sometimes, after a long and boring day on the road, convenience in an overnight stop is all that matters. So, staying in a parking lot of a retail store or mall may simply be the best alternative, particularly since there may be no campground nearby. And, if you put some effort into conserving your battery power, you should do just fine. Be certain that you obtain permission to camp on private property so that there will be no surprise interruptions.

- A great way to stay when visiting family members. There is nothing simpler than parking in a driveway when visiting grandchildren and other relatives.

Commonly Installed Equipment for Boondocking

To make boondocking work for you, a primary goal would be to make you as independent as possible from utility hookups for a period of time. In order to do this, and still keep most of the systems in the RV operational, the following is a list of suggested equipment:

- a converter/charger
- generator
- a built-in or portable inverter wired to the batteries which changes current from the batteries to alternating current to operate 120-volt appliances (tv, microwave, coffeemaker, toaster)
- RV refrigerator that is 12-volt DC/120-volt AC and propane
- a large freshwater tank
- large gray-water and black-water tanks
- two seven gallon propane tanks

A major consideration when boondocking is where to dump your tanks. In some cases it may be permissible to dump gray water tanks (sink and shower waste) on the ground. Black water (toilet waste) should be dumped into appropriate portable tanks or a nearby dump station. Many newer rigs contain macerator pumps.

Basically, the macerator grinds up solid waste so it can be drained from the black water tank through a water hose. We've found this to be quite convenient when boondocking because you can simply empty the black water tank into a portable tank and then transport the tank to a disposal station.

Helpful Hints

Depending on how long you expect to boondock, you will need to conserve on utilities. This is especially significant in terms of battery power and water.

Here are some useful hints:

- Try not to let the water run when you are not using it.
- Take a sponge bath in lieu of a shower.
- Use paper goods to dine if you dispose of them in a campsite fire pit.
- Grill outdoors as much as possible to eliminate the washing of pots and pans.
- Try to prepare multiple meals at one time to lessen clean-up times.
- Wipe off as much as you can from your dirty dishes before washing.

- Carry portable water tanks with you in case campground water sources are limited. If your campsite is close enough to a potable water source, you can refill your containers there or perhaps even hook up a hose to refill your tanks.

- If you boondock on a short-term basis, your batteries will recharge from your alternator when you drive and when you next plug in to shore power. You can recharge your batteries by using your generator, if you have one. It's best not to allow your batteries to drain fully before recharging them with the generator. We oftentimes run the generator during the day so that the batteries will be fully charged by evening. Many newer coaches have an ammeter. An ammeter can measure how big an amp load the system is drawing from your batteries at any one time and monitors your battery charging system.

- If you can afford it, solar panels are quite passive and green. Albeit they are expensive, they are a valuable addition to maintaining the battery charge. And, a solar power system will allow you to enjoy the benefits of clean, quiet, portable power that will last for many years with a minimum of maintenance. Just in case you are not familiar with this technology in an RV, solar panels convert the sun's rays into usable electricity. The electrical energy produced by the solar panel is transferred to a 12-volt battery and then can be converted to 110-volt AC power by an inverter. If you have the right set up in your rig, you should be able to camp just about anywhere there is sunshine.

Where To Boondock: Public Sites

This type of camping is usually found on Public Lands. Public campgrounds are usually run by a government agency. These campgrounds are mostly funded by tax dollars and are located in scenic areas or on land that may be set aside to preserve some aspect of the natural environment for present and future enjoyment.

THE BUREAU OF LAND MANAGEMENT

BLM areas include thirty-four National Wild and Scenic Rivers, one hundred thirty-six National Wilderness Areas, and so on. You can choose from 17,000 campsites at over four hundred different campgrounds, mostly in the western states.

Most of these campgrounds are primitive offering a picnic table and fire ring. Restrooms may or may not be available. The same situation applies to potable water. We've always found it best to camp in BLM camps on a self-contained basis. That way, all of your needs can be met during your stay.

Fees may range from five to ten dollars per night. Many of the camps charge no fee.

THE ARMY CORPS OF ENGINEERS

The Army Corps of Engineers Campgrounds are clean and well maintained and do offer the basic amenities: showers, restrooms, water, picnic tables, and fire rings. Some even have full hookups. The Corps has created over 4300 recreation areas at 450 lakes throughout the country. If you log onto their Lakes website, *(corplakes.usace.army.mil/visitors/)* you can explore camping descriptions including facilities.

FOREST SERVICE CAMPGROUNDS

Forest Service campgrounds are often situated in very beautiful places. Their website *(www.fs.fed.us)* has an excellent search mechanism, and you can request maps and brochures and learn about special programs.

RVers can choose from thousands of campsites at over 1700 locations. At the *recreation.gov* website you can easily search out a campground with your own preferences. Facilities are fully described and often times pictures are available. Additionally, you will find a map of the camp and some information about the area.

A word of caution is necessary here. Many of these camps were constructed in the 1940s and 1950s. There may be restrictions in place on the size of rigs permitted in the campground. Roads may be narrow and winding with low hung branches, which can make it a difficult passage with storage boxes and satellite dishes. Also, you may find that sites are too narrow for slideouts. It may be a good idea to take a walking tour of a camp so you can be assured that your rig will fit appropriately.

NATIONAL PARKS

The Park Service includes three hundred ninety areas comprising more than 84 million acres. Many of the National Parks have primitive or dry camping and are great stops for boondockers. You can easily explore the various parks at the NPS website (*nps.gov*).

HIGHWAY OVERLOOKS AND REST AREAS

How much more convenient could it be than to spend the night in a rest area on the Interstate. We have done it without ever experiencing difficulties.

Be aware that you'll need to get used to the sound of diesel eighteen-wheelers idling, possibly even right next to you. In addition, make certain that you see no signs that state " No Overnight Parking Permitted." Otherwise you may have an expected visitor (of the law enforcement nature) in the middle of the night.

For safety purposes if you intend to boondock in a rest area (or any parking area) choose a well-lit visible area. Try not to use rest area facilities at night. Also, make sure you lock all door and external compartments and do not leave valuables unattended.

Boondocking in Private Sites

Retail malls and chain stores usually have large well-lit parking lots. Examples of such lots include Wal-Mart, Kmart, and discount warehouses such as Sam's Club. Needless to say, make certain you have that all-important permission to camp. You can obtain that from store managers. You may even find that they have an electrical outlet available.

By the way, casinos are excellent places for convenience camping. Most do not prohibit overnight camping, especially if you patronize the establishment. You may actually find some tempting buffets available along with some interesting entertainment.

Finally, the easiest and quickest way to find boondock campsites is to do a search on Google. One of the sites you'll come up with is *freecampgrounds.com*. This site has an excellent search mechanism that allows you to seek out information by state. Information provided is detailed and you will find camper reviews of various locations.

CHAPTER 5: HANDLING THE INCIDENTALS

When you go off in your RV for extended periods of time, there are basic lifestyle details that must be attended to. Given the advancement in technology, dealing with these tasks has become much less challenging.

I am going to make a bold statement now: You absolutely must have a computer with you. I know that for some of you the thought of simply working on a computer is daunting. You are, however, never too old to learn. To learn more about the specific advantages of having the technology on the road, read Chapter 6.

Finances: Online Banking is the Best Way

These days, online banking services make life on the road much less stressful, especially when it comes to paying bills, managing accounts, and investing. There are, however, large numbers of you who absolutely refuse to conduct financial transactions online because of safety concerns. Be assured, it is safe! Banks use a 128-bit encryption that ensures that once the data has been encrypted, only the bank using the same encryption can view the data.

The very first thing I recommend is to arrange for all of your deposits to be made electronically. That includes Social Security, pension payments, annuity payments, and any other income. This is a safe way to bank.

I have been paying my bills online for many years. This process is basically a huge time saver. There are no stamps, envelopes, and Post Offices involved. And, wherever I travel, I can find some kind of Internet access.

I suggest you examine closely all of your monthly bills. Normally, mortgages, loans, utilities, credit card bills, and even insurance premiums can be paid electronically. You can pay directly through a bill payer, which may be your local bank, or you can have the bill automatically deducted from a checking account.

Some financial software companies offer a monthly bill pay service. For example, Quicken (*quicken.com*) offers a monthly service that starts at $9.95 per month. For that fee you can:

- Receive and view bills online
- Receive email notifications
- Pay bills with Quicken software
- Pay bills from up to ten accounts at different financial institutions
- Schedule payments up to one year in advance

- Transfer money between accounts

When paying bills through your bank, you can usually transfer an amount between accounts. You may even be able to have a bill charged to your credit card thereby reducing the number of bills you have to pay each month. If you are worried about your credit card balance, most companies offer online or telephone access.

An example of an online bank that is easy to work with is ING (*ingdirect.com*). They offer paperless checking, high interest rates, electronic transfers, and automatic deposits. All of these services are free.

In terms of investment management, I examine, make exchanges, redemptions, and anything else that I need to do at the investment firm's website. Remember, if you see the lock sign in the web address box, the website is encrypted. Basically, the means that it is very difficult for unauthorized people to view information traveling between two computers. It also means that the site has a certificate of authority that you can trust.

A Great ATM Suggestion When on the Road

I make extensive use of ATMs when on the road in my RV. As you may already know, it is a much simpler way to obtain cash than attempting to cash a check at an unfamiliar bank.

You should check into surcharge-free networks. Log onto AllPoint (*allpointnetwork.com*), or Alliance One (*allianceone.com*), or Co-op Financial (*opnetwork.org*).

One other good bit of advice is to check with your bank to see if they are a member of a surcharge-free network.

Mail

Having to decide how to handle mail delivery when you are away does require some thought. As a general rule, your Post Office will hold mail for a maximum of thirty days. So, if you are taking a short trip, the choice is simple.

If you are going to be away for a longer period of time, then you'll probably want to submit an official mail-forwarding request so that you can receive mail at the campground. This process can also be completed at the USPO website (*usps.com*). You should also indicate your expected date of return. If you do that, try to eliminate any non-essential mail. Be certain to submit the Post Office forwarding form at your seasonal location before you leave to reverse the process. Remember that all of this can be done online.

Then there is always the choice of having a friend or neighbor retrieve your mail and hold it for you. You can then make an arrangement to have important items sent to you, if you set-up camp in a particular location for a few days.

One of the benefits offered by the Good Sam Club (*goodsamclub.com*) is their mail forwarding service. For as little as ten dollars per month, they will forward your mail once per week or hold the mail for you. The Family Motor Coach Association (*fmca.com*) offers the same member benefit.

Medical Care and Prescriptions

When you are on the road for an extended period of time, be certain you are familiar with the particulars of your medical coverage. This is particularly salient if you require emergency care. If you are covered by Medicare, you are covered everywhere. Medicare supplement carries as well as most HMOs have their own specific provisions in place that you need to be aware of.

In terms of prescriptions, once your prescription is in the database of a pharmacy chain, you should be able to access it at any branch. Additionally, most of those pharmacies will call your doctor and obtain a renewal when the current prescription expires.

Taking Your Pet Along in the RV

If you're like me, and you have a pet that you consider close family member, it is difficult to leave that pet behind.

Unfortunately, some of us luck out in terms of having a pet that travels well. For example, I have a ten-year-old cat. If I put him in the motorcoach he is generally ok until I decide to start the engine. At that point, he becomes a raving beast. Of course, the salient point here is, according to the experts, is that you must begin pet travel experiences at an early age, so the animal has plenty of time to acclimate.

Here are some tips from the experts:

- It is best to start the pet with a few short test runs, especially if he is not used to traveling. Even spending time with him in a parked RV with the motor running is good.

- Cats should be kept in a carrier while traveling and dogs should be in a restraining harness in case of an accident.

- Feed your pet a bit less than normal so there is less likelihood of an upset stomach.

- It is probably a good idea to keep an ID tag on your pet if you are traveling to strange places in case he gets away.

- Never leave your pet in the RV in warm or hot weather unless you leave the AC on. Heat stroke is an important issue concerning your pet's health and it can be lethal to your pet. As you may know, heat stroke is due to an increase in body temperature.

Here is another very useful suggestion. Have you ever wondered what to do with your pet if you need a sitter for the day? Perhaps you'd like to spend some extended time away from your RV, or, maybe a family emergency has occurred. Check out Fetch Pet Care (*fetchpetcare.com*). Unlike kennels, these sitters are individuals in private homes. They are trained, fully insured, and have had a background check. If you have Internet access, simply type in your local zip code to see if any Fetch sitters are nearby.

Useful Checklists

Our friends the Engels (Chapter 3) have provided me with two very useful checklists. The first will expedite the stocking of the RV for trips. The second will provide you with a list of items to check both in the RV and home. Of particular interest are the items to be looked at when shutting down the home and RV after use. These procedures will afford you peace of mind whether you are coming or going.

SUPPLIES

Kitchen	Bathroom	Food		Misc.
Paper towels	Q-tips	Cereal	Olive Oil, mayo	Lighter
Dish detergent	Dove soap	Pasta & sauce	Tea/coffee	Rubber gloves
Saran	Detergent	Salt & Pepper	Half and half	Odor Pillows
Foil	Bounce	Peanut butter	Cremora	Trash bags
Paper plates	Wipes	Eggs. yogurt	Milk	Tools & drill
Ziplocks	T paste, floss	Bread, butter	OJ	Charcoal
Plastic-ware	Toilet Paper	Onions, veggies	Splenda, sugar	Moth Balls
Paper plates	Tissues	Fruit, jams	Popcorn	Ant repellant
Straws	Towels	Soup, spices	Cool Whip	Candles
Dish detergent	Repellant	Tuna/Chicken	Ice Cream	Maps, pen, paper
Hand sanitizer	Hair Spray	Mustard/ketchup	Bisquick	Clorox wipes
Bug spray	Shampoo	Meat, hot dogs	Wine	Umbrellas
Sponges	Condition-er	Potatoes, beans	Water	Flares/triangles
Trash bags	Deodorant	Salad, slaw	Coke	Spare keys
Latex gloves	**Medica-tion**	Rice	Cheese, crackers	**Rug**
	Makeup			Portable tank

CHECKLIST

Amuse-ment	House Shutdown	Truck	RV Shutdown Inside	RV Shutdown Outside
Bicycles	**Stop Mail**	Check oil	Furnace off	Step up
Biking gear	**Stop Paper**	Water levels	Air off	Antenna down
Laptop	Bedroom fan off	Check tires	Lights off	Awning up
Green fin. folder	Lamp Off	Check flashers	Secure inside	Bins locked
Batteries /adapters	Fill Birdfeeders	Head/tail-lights	Water pump off	Stow chairs/rug
Binocu-lars	Lock shed	Wiper fluid	Hot water off	Stow hoses
Camera/ printer	Water plants		Slide in	Stow cables
DVDs; CDs	Trash out		Windows closed	Fill water tank
Books	Heat/air set		Blinds down	Remove chocks
Instru-ments/ music	Clean fridge		Vents closed	Secure Bicycles
			Secure TV	Lock door
				Store port. tank

CHAPTER 6: PURSUING YOUR INTERESTS AND HOBBIES

As I indicated to you early on in this book, I look at the RV lifestyle as a <u>tool to implement your specific plan for retirement.</u> In consideration of retirement goals that include self-reinvention and self-rediscovery, your RV becomes very accommodating.

Again, if you consider that we living longer, healthier lives, there is time to experiment and try new things, especially if you have interests that you have a passion for.

So, let us explore some potential hobbies and interests that you can pursue in your RV.

A Major Interest: Visiting the Grandchildren

I've talked to many RVers about what was the most significant factor in the decision to become involved in the RV lifestyle. The general consensus was that their RV allowed them to visit grandchildren who reside in various locations around the country.

I have a daughter and granddaughter that live in Seattle, Washington, which is about three thousand miles from our home state of Connecticut. The trip across the country in our coach is always a wonderful experience. After making this trip the first time, we've been able to establish a routine of regular stops along the way. In effect, this increases our comfort level in that we know what to expect. And there is the anticipation of the joy (light) at the end of the tunnel!

Antiquing

If you have an interest in antiques, I'm sure you realize how very important it is that you be somewhat knowledgeable. Obviously, you do not want to be taken advantage of by unscrupulous dealers. There are a variety of printed resources available that will assist you with such things as appraisals, how to find the best prices, and what and when to buy and sell. A very useful guide is *The Unofficial Guide to Collecting Antiques*, by Sonia Weiss. Also, visit *antiqueresourcesinc.com*, which features timely discussions on current issues.

If you log onto *antiqueweek.com*, you can click a link that informs you of shows around the country.

Antiquesandthearts.com has a very useful calendar that keeps you informed of nationwide shows and auctions. This site is basically an online events newspaper.

Remember, it is always useful to stay in campgrounds with wireless Internet access so you can plan your schedule ahead of time.

Go to Quartzsite Arizona

Here's a great idea. If you have the time, the rig, and the resources, why not join the thousands of RVers each year that head to Quartzsite, Arizona during the months of January and February. Not only is the weather wonderful, but also you can camp in the beautiful southwest and attend the Quartzsite Shows and pursue hobby interests.

During an average year, shows include the Rock and Gem Show, the Sports, Vacation and RV Show, The Hobby and Craft Show, and the Rock & Roll Classic Car Show.

In case you are not familiar with camping in the area, 20,000 Bureau of Land Management campsites surround Quartzsite. The cost of the camping is free. It is important to note that the camping at these sites is dry. So, you will have to be self-contained. You may find as many as 100,000 campers present at times.

Digital Scrapbooking

Digital Scrapbooking utilizes computers, software, and digital photos to create beautiful scrapbook pages. How it works is, you store your photos in albums, or individually on your hard drive. Indeed, the process is very artistic. You can use any of the more popular software packages to edit your photos. Some of the more popular editing packages include:

- Adobe Photoshop
- Microsoft Digital Image Pro
- Ulead PhotoImpact
- Picasa (free from Google)
- Roxio Toast Titanium

Handcrafts

There are a wide variety of handcrafts amenable to the RV lifestyle. Those include the following:

- Weaving
- Watercolors
- Oil painting
- Acrylic design

Spend Time at a Library

Long past are the days when you went to the library to simply perform the mundane task of checking out a book. These days, libraries offer a lot more.

If you are spending time in an area near a library, be sure to check the events schedule. You can explore and pursue hobbies of all kinds.

Public libraries offer everything from language lessons, to various lecture series to classes on local history or even wildflowers. Many offer museum exhibits. You may even find listening booths to enjoy vast collections of music. It may be convenient for you to take your RV to the library and park in their lot for the day. If you are interested in local history, most reference rooms have books on regional and local topics covering history to folklore.

Here's a great example of the new trends in libraries.

In Phoenix, Arizona, the Burton Central Library will open its first coffee shop, the Open Book Café, joining several valley libraries that offer coffee bars. Other libraries in the same area offer patrons video games such as Guitar Hero and Yoga classes. Additionally, all branches in the Phoenix area computer classes and health lectures. The Glendale Arizona Library recently completed a lecture series with talks by holistic healers, metaphysical practitioners, and a hypnotherapist.

Most libraries offer large video collections these days. If you are camping in a particular location, it may be worth your while to take out a membership. The Burton Barr Library in Phoenix offers 11,000 video titles.

Take an RV Trip to Pursue a Hobby

As long as you have an RV, and presumably some extra time, why not travel to a destination to learn more.

Here's a great idea. Why not travel to Ghost Ranch (*ghostranch.org*) in Santa Fe, New Mexico. In addition to all of the natural beauty surrounding you, a wide variety of art and culture course are available for enrollment. Some of the courses are offered in conjunction with Elderhostel.

Course offerings include: quilting, blacksmithing, pottery, archaeology, meditation, opera and music.

Folkschool.org, situated in the beautiful mountains of North Carolina, offers about 450 courses. The curriculum includes music, photography, blacksmithing, sculpturing, calligraphy, gardening, woodcarving and a great deal more. The school even has its own campground that is open year-round. It features twelve RV sites and six tent sites. Hookups are available and a bathhouse with toilets and showers is located onsite. You can elect to participate in their meal plan or simply prepare your own meals.

If you are looking for festivals and special events to attend, visit *festivals.com*. Here you can seek out events by subjects that include arts, culture, motorsports, music, and even kid's stuff. You can also search by state. There's even a clickable map with statewide events listed.

Roadsideamerica.com is another online guide that emphasizes offbeat tourist attractions. So, for example, if you are interested in unusual museums and you able to travel to the Wisconsin Dells, visit the Museum of Historic Torture Devices. Or, you can visit the Dinosaur Walk Museum in Pigeon Forge, Tennessee and walk among life-size sculptures.

Writing

Writing is a great hobby to pursue in an RV. Take it from one who knows. My first book was written almost in its entirety in my while on the road in my Class A motorhome.

Now I'm not intimating that you too should write a book, unless you want to. Many people write books about their interests and hobbies. However, if you have always had the desire to write, the RV lifestyle can be very accommodating and stimulating while gazing out over the passing panoramas.

If you are interested in writing as a hobby, then you will need to think about how you want to pursue it. That is, do you want to write for fun while on the road and keep collections, or, are you desirous of getting published. Of course you can self-publish which may be of interest to you if you are publishing more for fun.

I've included some suggestions for those of you who would like get into freelance writing. These are ideas presented by Jan and Gordon Groene in their book entitled *Living Aboard Your RV.*

- Set a daily writing goal. If you are on the road maintain Internet access and carry along a high quality printer

- Buy a copy of Writer's Market (*writersmarket.com*). This will help you locate sources to query with your writing and tell you how to publish.

- Write consistently and persistently. If you would like to be published, send out proposals and query letters on a regular basis

- Find your own niche. Editors seek out writers who focus on a specialty. You will stand out in a crowded marketplace.

I also suggest that you look into starting a blog. A blog is considered to be an online sales hub. And, you can start one for free on Google's Blogger site *(blogger.com)*. Over time, you can create traffic patterns with this blog. That could ultimately translate into income.

CHAPTER 7: WORKAMPING

There is absolutely nothing wrong with working during your "Third Age." There, I said it! Many of you may think that one cannot be retired and be employed at the same time. To that I say, remember that we are attempting to rediscover ourselves. You may feel that you've developed a new sense of purpose because you are trying something that you've always wanted to do.

If you are not certain of the meaning of the term "Workamping," simply look at the word itself. The first thing that comes to mind is working while you camp. Basically, that is it! According to the folks at *workamper.com*, Workamping includes any activity that involves the exchange of man/women hours for anything of value. The term does not specifically relate to working in a campground.

It is important to understand that the term "Workamping" does not necessarily pertain to retired people. In fact, *workamping.com* states that the average age of Workampers is fifty-three. So, you may be the adventurous type and adore traveling in your RV and moving about the country and do not wish to live in one location.

There are a variety of reasons to Workamp. You may simply want to supplement your retirement income to support a nearly full-time RV lifestyle. Additionally, this is another aspect of the RV lifestyle that is cost effective. If you have a job as a campground host, and you enjoy meeting people, you may only have to work a few hours a day. In turn, you may be remunerated with a free campsite and hookups. It is even possible that you may be able to secure this type of job in one of our beautiful National or State Parks. I've met lots of very satisfied hosts in a variety of settings over the years, who all agree that this Workamper job really does support a satisfying retirement lifestyle.

Many people today are interested in reinventing themselves in terms of working. A major consideration here is deciding upon how much time you would like to devote to working, and how much time you would like to spend Rving. Many Workamping jobs are seasonal, so in essence, you should have plenty of time to enjoy your RV travels between jobs. Working out of your coach or trailer can be a great option if you are thinking or retiring early. The point is, that you have chosen a wonderful style of living that can reinforce any kind of part-time or full-time work (paid or volunteer).

Many Workamper jobs today are available in the Outdoor Hospitality Industry. Singles and couples are in constant demand at the following locations:

- Campgrounds
- Resorts
- National parks
- Marinas
- Forests
- Theme parks
- Lodges
- State parks
- Ski resorts
- Youth camps
- Wildlife preserves
- RV parks
- Guest ranches
- Historical sites
- Museums

Here is an extended list of possible jobs for Workampers, as taken from *workampers.com*:

Campgrounds & RV Parks (commercial & government):
- Activity Director/Entertainer
- Camp Host
- Assistant Manager
- Manager
- Off-season Caretaker
- Maintenance Supervisor
- Relief Manager
- Membership Sales
- Naturalist/Interpreter
- Contract Gate Attendant
- Volunteer Park Attendant
- Camp Host Coordinator

Theme Parks/Amusement Parks/Tourist Attractions/Circuses/ Carnivals
- Retail Sales
- Ride Operator
- Tram Driver

- Security
- Food Service
- Ticket Office
- Actor/Performer
- Musician
- Groundskeeper
- Petting Zoo Attendant

Dude Ranches/Outdoor Outfitters/Lodges/Cabins/Motels/ Retreats

- River Guide
- Canoe Livery Driver
- Wrangler
- Cooks
- Food Service
- Housekeeper
- Reservations/Front Desk
- Housekeeping Supervisor
- Off-season Caretaker
- Grounds Supervisor
- Livestock Tender

Motorsports

- Usher
- Ticket Stubber
- Parking Attendant
- Security
- Concessions
- Souvenir Sales
- Campground Attendant
- Campground Manager

Business & Income Opportunities

- RV park snack bar for lease
- Campgrounds For Sale/Lease
- Map Sales
- Souvenir/Award Sales
- Power Tool Distributor
- Aerial Photo Sales
- Forwarding/Message Service Sales

Career Opportunities

- Director of Education
- General Manager

- Operations Manager
- Park Management Team
- Assistant Manager

Other

- RV Delivery Driver
- Utility Inspector
- Campground Inspector
- Park Map Sales
- Field Rep
- Kiosk Sales
- Gift Shop clerk
- Golf Course Attendant
- Tour Guide
- RV Technician
- RV Sales
- Estate/Property Sitter

Kampgrounds of America (*koa.com*)

A great way to maintain an income and see the country is to become a Workamper for KOA. According to KOA, eighty percent of its Workampers are between the ages of fifty-one and eighty. Fifty-seven percent work between four and six months per year for KOA. At the time of this writing there are 460 locations around the country with a variety of opportunities available. The company offers perks for its Workampers including a $10,000 cash prize. The website offers a database of jobs at the campgrounds. Check it out at *koa.com/workatkoa*.

Working From the RV

Remember, as a Workamper you can work from the comfort of your RV. So, you may be able to run an online business or tele-commute. Here are some thoughts from an article in *Family Motor Coach Magazine* (12/07) if you are fulltiming and have interest in part-time or full-time work. This information is especially helpful if you are considering working for someone else.

- Consider your space requirements. If you plan to set up an office in your RV, do you have the space you will need to work? You may need to obtain a computer desk.

- Think about climate considerations. If you have a work contract that requires that you work in extreme heat or cold, or during hurricane season, can you deal with that?
- Know before you go. Sometimes, preliminary discussions do not present a clear picture of the employment details. Careful research can be important here so that time is not wasted.
- Are you provided a campsite as part of the job benefits? Even if you are not, it is a good idea to check out the campground ratings thoroughly. You can go to a website such as *rvparkreviews.com* or check ratings in a variety of campground directories. Environment around the campsite may be important to you, such as the presence of rail lines, power lines, or Interstates.

You will need to need to ascertain information on access to utilities, security, and proximity to shopping needs.

If you are looking for a to job to make use of a specific skill, log onto the following websites:

Kellyservices.com is a nationwide temporary employment agency offering benefits that accumulate and follow you from job to job. If you accept work from a temporary employment agency, ask the agency to fax or e-mail your records to the office closest to your destination. You will then have your paperwork completed and a good recommendation waiting for you when you arrive. By the way, these temporary agencies may very well have jobs available for engineers, draftsmen, and a host of other professions.

Monster.com maintains a huge database of jobs, while jobs are listed by city on *craigslist.org*.

Networking Helps

Sometimes in life it is who you know that means a great deal. Seems like I've heard that before. In the case of networking for a job, the development of contacts, and or the exchange of information can be of great benefit in finding a job while in on the road.

For example, let's assume that you are interested in working in an RV park, but you do not know much about it. One thing you can do is to make an appointment with the management of the park you are staying to find out about jobs in RV parks. Most people who work in the parks are delighted to share information with you. In fact, I've found that much of the time, campground personnel are Workampers themselves.

Another useful tip is to get involved in an Internet RV discussion group or blog such as *RV.Net*. A recent search produced a large variety of topics related to Workamping positions.

Make it a practice to ask other Rvers about their jobs. A lead to a job opening could readily result. You will find that most Rvers are readily willing to help others.

Preparing Your Resume' for Workamping

It is probably unlikely that you will need a detailed resume' for most Workamping positions. However, it is certainly a professional way to apply for a position and indicate to a potential employer that you are the right person for the job.

There are a variety of software templates available, many of which are included with most word processing programs. You can also check resources at a local library. It is very important that you do a thorough spell-check and grammar check on the finished document. It may even be helpful to have another person proofread your resume. Normally, you will want to have the length be no longer than one page.

The following is a suggested list of categories for you to include in your resume. The categories should be in capital letter and bold type.

- personal identification information
- work objective
- work experience
- specific work skills and experience with technology
- education
- hobbies and interests
- references

Events within the categories are usually listed chronologically with current activities listed first.

CHAPTER 8: CAN I LIVE IN THIS THING FULLTIME?

In case you are not familiar with the terminology, fulltiming in an RV is just that. You've given up your domicile and your primary residence has become mobile. At least one million Americans have pulled up stakes, sold their homes, and live in an RV.

Pat and Dennis Swann were getting along with money from Social Security and pensions to live a modest lifestyle in their Seattle area home when they retired a number of years ago. But, there was not a great deal of room for extras, such as travel. According to Pat, they could not afford more than taking two or three weeks of vacation each year.

The Swanns could have downsized to a smaller home or moved into a cheaper area. Instead, they rid themselves of their home altogether and bought a recreational vehicle. Pat has indicated that they would never again buy a house.

For some, fulltiming is a sense of adventure. Many ardent fulltimers become gypsies. Any excuse to travel will suffice. It may be an opportunity to see places they might not otherwise see including historic trails, national parks, big cities, and special rallies. Again, this may be an integral part of your plan for retirement. It is an avenue for self-reinvention. A benefit for some that accompanies this plan is a lifestyle that may be free of encumbrances of a stationary home.

For others, fulltiming may be an economic necessity. Given the nature of the uncertain economic times we live in, with recession a possibility, this RV lifestyle may be more affordable.

Whatever your reasons are for considering this lifestyle, there are many considerations, choices, and even tradeoffs that you may be faced with when making this decision. Examples include:

- Can you realistically coexist with your mate in somewhat confined quarters? Do you have interests in common? Will you get in each other's way? Space can be an important consideration.

- You will have to choose an RV that you can afford.

- Have you the financial resources to enjoy the RV lifestyle? If not, are you prepared to offset the costs by working on the road (see the chapter in this book on Workamping)?

- Does your medical plan cover you while you are on the road? Will you be able to fill any necessary prescriptions? You may need supplemental insurance.

- Provisions for receiving your mail will have to made. Possibilities include arranging mail forwarding, or perhaps having a relative accept delivery. This is especially critical when it comes to paying bills. Remember, it perfectly safe to pay bill online.

- Keeping in touch with family and friends on the road is another important consideration. (See the chapter on Keeping In Contact).

- Should you take a pet along? If not, what is the alternative?

- What can you do about personal possessions that you cannot take with you in the RV? Many people put their stuff in storage or leave it with family members. It is most important that you have a realistic outlook here: A dramatic change takes from your previous word of walk-in-closets, three car garages, and personal swimming pools.

Do you have a personality that is compatible with fulltime RVing?

Malia Lane, a writer for *fulltimerver.com,* suggests some things for you to think about in the privacy of your own home before you trade it in for an RV. After all, fulltiming is a major life decision and must be considered carefully.

First, are you comfortable with change? Can you tolerate a regular diet of the unknown and the unplanned?

Second, there is the issue whether you need routine in your life. Certainly you can create your own lifestyle, but traveling is mostly about change, staying open and flexible, and experiencing new things. Much of this depends on how much you value continuity.

Do you enjoy being around adventurous folks? These people may generally love to converse and share their experiences.

Are you a shy person? RVers are friendly people. You may value your privacy, which can become complicated when you are sitting outside under your RV awning.

Sometimes personal security can become a consideration. You may need to ask yourself if the RV lifestyle can offer enough stability. Remember, you will not have a house and the accompanying possessions.

How much RV maintenance are you willing to do? Staying on the road safely means checking and replacing things as necessary. You will need to maintain your fresh water tanks, hot water heater, and change water, AC, and furnace filters regularly.

What About Claiming Residency

Without a permanent address claiming a state of residency may become somewhat challenging if you are a full-timer.

In order to keep a valid driver's license, purchase tags for your vehicle and register to vote, you need to show some proof of living in most states. Some documentation is needed to show physical evidence.

Many fulltimers enjoy living a freewheeling lifestyle on the road and do indeed give up their primary residence. Most of these RVers use a relative's address or even that of a mail forwarding service, according to the Good Sam Club. They recommend using the address of one of your children and conduct all of your business through that address. Some vary in whether they recognize a mail forwarding service.

Cost Saving Strategies

During these times of fuel pricing volatility, some cost saving suggestions seem appropriate.

When you think about the average temperatures in San Diego, California, the city does indeed, seem ideal. Daytime temperatures average from sixty-five to seventy-seven degrees. So, heating and cooling costs in an ideal climate such as San Diego, may be minimal.

For those of us who travel in less than optimum climates, those heating and cooling costs become more of a concern. Therefore, when you are shopping for an RV, concentrate your efforts on a rig that is well insulated. For example, are the windows single or dual pane? Also, are the window treatments heavy duty enough to keep the indoor temperature stable? It may be worth the expense to install insulated window treatment in your rig if you will be spending time in more extreme climates.

If you are staying in campground that includes electricity in your nightly or monthly fee, be certain to switch the refrigerator and the hot water heater over to electric.

In an effort to conserve fuel, be certain to dump the holding tanks and keep the fresh water storage tanks at a minimum to reduce your overall weight. Every pound makes a difference.

As mentioned previously in the chapter on Boondocking, you can live without hookups. Many fulltimers do. Solar panels, batteries, and inverters do help.

CHAPTER 9: TECHNOLOGY & INTERNET ACCESS IN THE RV: KEEPING CONNECTED

During a large portion of my teaching career, I was a public school technology teacher. During that period of time I taught my students that the tools of technology could be thought of as a way to make life easier. As you will see in the following discussion, that specific advantage that the tools of technology can provide becomes even more pronounced during our retirement years in an RV.

Internet Access

In my second book, *Technology & Your Retirement Lifestyle: Tools For The New You*, I discuss ways that those tools can enhance your retirement lifestyle. It is significant to note that the tools of technology can support your mobile lifestyle. The question is: How can those tools help you while in the RV? If so, do I need any special equipment? You will also need to consider space requirements in your RV. Space will need to be available for a desktop computer and possibly a printer. Certainly, a laptop computer would help here.

When you are traveling, the most immediate need for technology is access to the Internet. A most common concern is how to I obtain that access? There are a variety of alternatives, most of which can be utilized by RVers.

The following is a list of suggested locations to log onto a computer.

- public libraries
- Internet cafes
- airports
- hot spots (truck stops, campgrounds)

WI-FI AND HOTSPOTS

A Wi-Fi enabled device such as a computer, game console, cell phone, MP3 player of PDA can connect to the Internet through a wireless network. The coverage of one or more interconnected access points is called a hotspot. The area a hotspot can cover can comprise an area as small as a single room to a large area many square miles covered by overlapping access points. A good source for finding hotspots is the

wi-fihotspotsdirectory.com. The site lists a searchable database of wireless Internet locations from all over the world that are frequently updated.

Another directory of free Wi-Fi hotspots is *wififreespot.com*. The site is free to users because advertising supports it.

At campgrounds, the speed and range of a hotspot will vary depending on the specific Wi-Fi network and configuration at the campground. Additionally, most campground directories will provide information regarding Wi-Fi availability in the campground. A good suggestion is to check with the reservations clerk at a particular campground regarding the level of service at campsites.

During my most recent trips, I've found that most full service campgrounds offer wireless Internet access. Sometimes this service is free, while at other times you may have to pay a small daily service charge. Since it is necessary for me to be online when I travel, I usually check ahead to inquire about service availability. A helpful tip when selecting a site at a campground is to request a location that is near the wireless antenna. This will help to assure that you will have a strong signal. If you are required to pay a service charge, check the long-term rates in addition to the daily rates. Often times it makes more sense to sign on with the longer-term rate, as it may be less expensive.

An important consideration with wi-fi is that every hotspot is different. That is; you cannot be quite sure of the reception.

Remember, in an RV park, hotspots are shared. Bandwidth may be limited if there are a large number of people using it. When you think about it, this situation is similar to the old party-line system, when you would get pretty angry if one party was hogging the line all the time. If you are lucky, and there only a few campers in the park, you may be able obtain a fast connection and download as much as you desire.

Most laptop computers come equipped with 802.11b/g (wi-fi) capability suitable for RV Internet access. I've been using this technology for years with a great deal of success.

WI-FI THROUGH YOUR CELL PHONE

If you are a fulltimer, you may be desirous of having Internet access all of the time wherever you are. That would include access at any RV park whether in a city or remote area, as long as there is cellular service available.

One way to do this would be through your cellular provider with companies like Verizon Wireless, Sprint, AT&T or T-Mobile. Make absolutely certain that you understand your provider's terms of service. For example, at the time of this writing, Verizon's broadband plan is $59.99 per month and gets you five gigabytes of bandwidth. If you go over, you will be charged $.49 for every extra megabyte. It is important that you understand your usage, especially if you view online videos.

In its simplest form, you use the cell phone, PDA, or integrated PDA/cell phone display screen to retrieve e-mail and do web browsing. Internet access is through the wireless provider, using one of their various monthly plans.

Your cell phone may also be used as a modem for RV Internet access. The way this works is the cell phone is connected to the computer via a USB cable, infrared or Bluetooth. This method offers you the opportunity to have a larger display. You will also need to make certain that your cell phone is web-enabled.

Another handy option for Internet access is an "Aircard." This is a device that will enable you to have Internet access without having to rely on hot spot availability, access to a phone line, or sharing a wired connection at a job site. You will need to have a service plan, normally through your cell phone service provider, that allows you access the Internet with your Aircard.

SATELLITE RV INTERNET ACCESS

Another way to access the Internet is through a personal satellite system. The antenna is either mounted automatically on the roof or manually situated on a separate tripod unit that can be positioned within the campsite.

A major advantage of the satellite option is that in most situations you will be able to camp in wilderness parks and still have Internet access, as long as a clear view of the southern sky.

Most systems are comprised of a small 18" or 20" dish, a receiver, a remote control and various installation goodies.

Manufacturers of the automatic-mount products include MotoSAT's Datastorm, DirecStar, and Ground Control. Prices, with installation can range from $5000 - $5500. There is a monthly charge of $99.00.

Costs for manually mounted units can run about $1300 to $1700 and higher for packages with different types of satellite aiming devices. Monthly plans may run from $59 and up.

You will have to consider how important the differences between the two systems are to you. Certainly, automatic systems are easier to deploy. The manual mounts need to be set up and disassembled. It is suggested that one half an hour is the amount of time required. The mount will need to be transported. It should be noted that the equipment is not small.

Finally, you will need to think about the price difference. A key factor here is how often you will need and use your RV Internet access.

Ways to Utilize Technology in the RV

Have you heard of the new terminology called "social networking"? Just in case you have not, the networking process provides a collection of various ways for people to interact, such as audio and video conferencing, messaging, e-mail, file sharing, blogging, discussion groups and so on. Basically, social networking has revolutionized the way we communicate and share information with each other in today's society.

E-mail

I have been e-mailing for at least twenty years. Much of that electronic correspondence has been done in campground offices (beginning with the dialup process) and in the comfort of my RV. I sincerely believe in the value of email, as it is less expensive and faster than snail mail, and, less intrusive than a phone call. It also is more comforting for those of us who are phone phobic. Additionally, the turn around time for a response is much faster. I am constantly e-mailing pictures when I travel in order to share our experiences.

Networking Sites

Networking sites are what most people are familiar with when you refer to social networking. *Myspace.com* has become increasingly popular among the older generation. *Facebook.com* is, at the moment, involving a smaller population and seems a bit less wild and easier to navigate.

Then there are a variety of other sites that cater to specific groups of people: *Eons.com* is geared toward the boomer population. One of their major goals is to encourage its members to start groups in an effort to fuel passions and interests. There are also a variety of games offered that you can play solo or with others. *Gather.com* is also an adult membership site that encourages the pursuit of your interests and hobbies.

Social networking is a great way to connect with things and people that bring happiness and or learning into your life.

.

Blogs

A web log (blog for short) is basically a journal that is posted on the Internet. It can be restricted to certain people with access limited by password, or, it can be open to the public.

There are at least 100 million blogs out there on just about any subject. The writer or "blogger" may offer first hand experience on a subject that hopefully will be accurate. The information offered includes commentaries or news regarding the topic at hand.

For Rvers, blogs can be a great way for friends and families to share travel information. Some blogs are forums with many people providing input. In a sense, some blogs are similar to travelogues, taking you to destinations that you've never been to.

There are several good blog search engines that point you in the right direction. However, you will need to be specific in your search to find exactly what you are looking for. Here are some suggestions:

- *blogsearch.google.com*
- *technorati.com*
- *RVtravel.com* – click on RV travel blog section
- *travellerspoint.com*

- *MyTripJournal.com* – offers a choice of countries
- *RV.net*

If you would like to start a blog, it is a great way to promote the writer in all of us, and maybe even to begin a new hobby. A fair amount of your time will be required to post entries and responses. *blogger.com* (Google) and *wordpress.com* offer help to get you up and running very quickly.

Audio and Video Conferencing

Since so many of us have high speed Internet connectivity these days, and the cost of personal video teleconference components has become more affordable, more of us are videoconferencing on our home computer. The cost of a webcam is reasonable and, if you have an up to date computer, conferencing becomes easy.

There are a number of free chat programs that make videoconferencing more accessible. As I am on the road quite often, I am desirous of keeping in contact with my family and friends on a regular basis. With the aforementioned availability of wi-fi in most campgrounds, coffee shops, and rest areas, connectivity for audio or video conferencing becomes easy. By the way, you can log onto *wififreespot.com* for a comprehensive list of hotspots.

I most often use Skype (*skype.com*) for conferencing. Typical of most free downloads you can make free Skype-to-Skype calls to anyone in the world. If you do not have a webcam you can still audio with others. You also have the capability to group chat. Skype even offers a low cost plan to call ordinary phones and mobiles.

I also use iChat (*apple.com/ichat/)*. Apple offers glitzy features such as video backdrops, photo booth effects, photo slideshows, and movies that can all be shared. IChat works with AIM, a large instant messaging community. This allows both PC and Mac users to chat.

Remember that to videoconference you will need either a video camera with Firewire capability or a webcam. Logitech (*logitech.com*) makes webcams that cost as little as thirty dollars at the time of this writing.

Global Positioning System (GPS)

A GPS is an indispensable tool for the RVer, especially if you are on the road for long periods of time. For the most part, you can leave the road atlas at home. All you need is an address. Simply enter information onto your GPS receiver if you do need help with those directions. You also have the capability of doing cool stuff like gathering positions at regular times and showing your position on a moving map display.

You can choose a GPS that is permanently installed in your vehicle, or one that is portable, or even a hand held unit. Expect to spend from one hundred dollars up to one thousand dollars.

GPS units can provide the following important information for the RVer:

- the time and mileage to a destination
- show you the name of the next town
- find rest areas along the way
- provide a summary of the trip

CHAPTER 10: VOLUNTEERING ON THE ROAD

Why Volunteer?

Remember that all-important retirement plan we discussed in Chapter 1. A key component for many retirees these days is volunteerism. An excellent tool to support this goal is your RV. You are free to move about this land to explore the diverse opportunities that await you.

Oftentimes you may be able to place yourself in a position while being near your family. Tom and Nancy volunteered in Prescott National Forest to be near Nancy's mother while she adjusted to a new living situation in nearby Prescott, Arizona. As campground hosts they were able to set their own hours. They had plenty of time to visit regularly with Nancy's mother during the week. Additionally, Tom signed up as a mentor with Big Brothers/Big Sisters and worked on a site development committee for the local Natural History Center by conducting research surveys.

People volunteer for a variety of reasons. Usually, a major influence is the desire to help others. Traditionally, volunteering has been viewed as an altruistic tendency even being construed as a form of charity.

There is a school of thought that considers volunteering as an exchange. That is, although you may be the person with ability to help today, indeed you may be the recipient of someone else's volunteer effort tomorrow.

Then there are other benefits that are motivators. Many volunteers feel the need to give back and share with others their life skill experiences.

Examples of Real RV Volunteerism

CAMPGOUND HOST OPPORTUNITIES

National Parks *(nps.gov)* or USDA Forest Service *(www.fs.fed.us/fsjobs/jobs_volunteers)* - Hundreds of National, State and Provincial agencies attempt to recruit volunteers. The most obvious are the National Park Service, Bureau of Land Management, Corps of Engineers, Forest Service, and the U.S. Fish and Wildlife Service. Hours can range from ten to thirty hours per week and commitments can range from one to six months. The most common volunteer positions are campground hosts, followed by interpreters. There are also office jobs available as well as jobs requiring physical labor. Benefits for volunteer positions can include an RV site or housing, stipends, transportation, utilities, propane, uniforms and training.

In fiscal year 2005, 137,000 volunteers donated 5.2 million hours to the national parks. VIPs (Volunteer in Parks) came from all over the world to help preserve and protect America's natural and cultural heritage for the enjoyment of generations to come. The National Park Service website maintains a database of volunteer opportunities that you can search by state. There are links to the USA Freedom Corps, International Volunteer-In-Parks, as well as the Artists-In-Residence programs.

Volunteer Rvers have successfully parlayed their volunteer experiences into paid positions. Jim worked two seasons at Acadia National Park in Maine as a volunteer ranger. The summer following he was hired as a park ranger.

I also recommend that you log onto the *volunteer.gov/gov* website which displays public sector volunteer opportunities. It is a partnership among the U.S. departments of Agriculture, Defense, Interior, Veterans Affairs, U.S. Army Corps of Engineers, and U.S.A. Freedom Corps. The goal here is to present you with an easy-to-use web portal with a useful search mechanism.

Volunteer Camp Hosting in State Parks - Among the volunteer positions here are also campground activity directors. The director schedules and conducts entertainment and activities in the campground for campers. Responsibilities for camp hosts include guest assistance, security, and helping park staff with various other tasks. The host may also be required to:

- greet new visitors
- hand out literature
- answer questions about the area
- be alert to campers needs and complaints

For a list of volunteer positions in state parks nationwide go to the Happy Vagabonds website (*happyvagabonds.com/*).

U.S. Army Corps of Engineers (orn.usace.army.mil/volunteer/) – he Corps Clearinghouse website provides information about volunteer opportunities available on the vast 12 million acres of land and water that it cares for.

These include:

- trail building and maintenance
- campground hosting
- building wildlife habitats
- presenting educational programs

- writing and editing material for publication
- developing computer programs
- photography
- building and maintaining archery ranges
- giving interpretive tours of dam sites

The website offers a searchable database of volunteer openings. Again, many of these openings offer free campground accommodations in exchange for your services.

U.S. Department of the Interior's Bureau of Land Management – (www. blm.gov/volunteer/) - The Bureau manages 261 million acres. Each year over 20,000 Americans volunteer their time and talent. BLM volunteers enjoy a seasonal or full-time position. Most of the lands are located primarily in the Western part of the United States. Their mission is to help sustain the health, diversity, and productivity of these public lands for present and future generations. Examples of opportunities include:

- restoration of streams, wildlife habitats, and ecosystems
- serving as a river ranger
- sharing your talents as an educator or youth group leader by conducting field trips, and visitor center programs

- update mineral survey maps
- operate office equipment
- computerize information for resource management plans
- assist with soil and water conservation projects
- plans trees and shrubs in fire-damaged areas
- write, edit or take photographs for publications
- assist with care of wild horses
- much more

HABITAT FOR HUMANITY *(habitat.org)*

A volunteer experience that fits perfectly in to the RV lifestyle is Habitat. Just in case you do not know, the goal of Habitat is to "eliminate poverty housing and homelessness from the world, and to make decent shelter a matter of conscience and action."

They have built more than 225,000 houses around the world, providing more than one million people with safe, decent, affordable shelter. This is accomplished through volunteer labor and donations of money and materials. Houses are built and rehabilitated and sold to partner families at no profit and financed with affordable loans. So as you can see, Habitat is not a giveaway program. The average cost of a home can be as little as $800 in developing countries to an average of $60,000 in the United States.

So, you may be wondering how you can get involved with your RV. Habitat For Humanity RV Care-A-Vanner program offers anyone with an RV the opportunity to make a difference and, have fun while doing it. This program welcomes people of all ages and all walks of life who are ready to "pick up a hammer."

The RV Care-A-Vanner program is a unique program and no experience is necessary to participate. In the past these volunteers have done construction, roofing, interior and finish work. There are even tasks for non-builders to assist in such as office work or errand completion. The length of the day is usually six to seven hours with breaks for meals.

Team members in this program pay their own expenses, which may be tax deductible. The host affiliates usually arrange for RV parking. You can expect at least minimal electric hookups for your rig with access to water and a dump station nearby. Team members often have the opportunity to work alongside local volunteers and future homeowners. If you have the time and inclination, you may even be able to partner with team affiliates around the country to promote awareness of poverty housing and homelessness by speaking to churches and civic groups and local media.

To find out more information regarding available openings click on the "build listing" link at the Habitat RV Care-A-Vanners website.

Virtual Volunteerism

Just in case you are not familiar with the terminology, When you virtually volunteer, you perform all of your responsibilities from the comfort of your RV. Needless to say, it is very important that you are able to get online when necessary.

Serviceleader.org suggests the following criteria to be successful as a virtual volunteer:

●Be certain that you are prepared to fulfill the commitment you are making.

●It is important that you have regular and consistent access to the Internet.

●Do you communicate well via the written word?

●Are you comfortable working on your own without direct supervision?

●Deadlines are important.

•Do you answer your e-mails promptly?

•A virtual assignment requires a certain level of concentration and intensity.

All of the following organization offer opportunities to virtually volunteer:

•Literacy Volunteers (*literacyvolunteers.org*) – promotes literacy for adults and their families

•Volunteer Match (*voluntermatch.org)* – dedicated to helping everyone find a great place to volunteer

•Retired Executives *(score.org)* – specializing in volunteer counselors for small businesses nationwide

•SeniorNet (*seniornet.org)* – a variety of nationwide virtual opportunities available

•Servenet (*servenet.org)*

•*Serviceleader.org* – volunteer opportunities that specialize in helping non-profits, schools, and government offices

•Nabuur (*nabuur.com*) – site that connects volunteers with opportunities in developing countries that have Internet access

• *Elderwisdomcircle.org* – Cyber-Grandparents connect with people in their teens, twenties, and thirties for personal anonymous advice

• Lawyers Without Borders (*lwob.org*) – volunteer lawyers from around the globe who stand ready to offer pro bono service to international projects and initiatives

• *Icouldbe.org* – volunteers mentor underprivileged teens online and help them with educational and career goals

• *Usafreedomcorps.gov* - a great way for baby boomers to get involved with a campaign aimed at 77 million boomers via a great search mechanism

Examples of virtual volunteer positions include telementoring, teletutoring, research, Web page creation, database design and much more.

CHAPTER 11: LEARNING WHILE RVING

By now, you are certainly aware that we are living longer and healthier lives. So why not make the most of all that time. It seems that we have the time to experiment with new things and perhaps even rediscover our passions. And, the learning process never ends. You can easily continue that process in the comfort of your RV if you know where the resources are. You can also travel to locations that offer special continuing education programs. So there is yet another way to see that your RV is a tool to implement the goals of that all-important plan for retirement.

The following examples illustrate ways that you can continue to learn and grow.

Local Adult Education, Recreation Center, and Senior Center Activities

If you are a full-timer or even a part-timer and you spend several months at a time in one location, you may be able to take courses in an adult education program, recreation center, or even a senior center that is affiliated with city or town where you are camping. The ability to do this mostly depends on residence requirements. The cost of enrollment in these courses is minimal. Here is a list of some of the courses that are offered by the various programs:

- technology coursework
- creative writing
- Chinese cooking
- classic novels
- yoga
- candle making
- foreign language basic conversation

Distance Learning

Just in case you do not know what it is, distance learning involves taking courses virtually. That is, you do not actually go to classes but complete required coursework on the computer. Online programs can readily lead to bachelor's degree, a master's degree, and even a doctor of philosophy.

The two most important considerations here are that you obviously need to have some skills in using a computer and the Internet. Experience with word processing is a must. Additionally, you will need to have access to the Internet when you need it. See Chapter 6 for a discussion on the various connectivity choices available to you while on the road. As I indicated previously, wireless Internet is readily available at many campgrounds. With a detailed campground directory and a call to the campground, you should be able to get online.

The University of Phoenix (*phoenix.edu*) offers a wide variety of degrees with full accreditation. This institution is very highly rated by the Wall Street Journal. You can select from programs in business, health care, criminal justice, education and technology. Certainly you do not have to matriculate. You can enroll in courses for pleasure.

The UCLA extension program (*uclaextension.edu*) offers hundreds of online courses. Here you can even acquire skills for the purpose of beginning a new career. Fields of study here include: Architecture and Interior Design, Business, Entertainment Studies, Journalism, Landscape Architecture, Public Health, Legal Issues, and Fitness Instruction.

Other great resources for distance learning are Yahoo Distance Learning (*dir.yahoo.com/ Education/Distance_Learning)* and *geteducated.com.*

Some informative books include:

1. *Peterson's Guide to Distance Learning Programs*
2. *Thorsen's Guide to Campus Free College Degrees*
3. *The Best Distance Learning Schools*

Study a Foreign Language

If you've ever had an inner desire to learn conversational skills in a foreign language, you can do so in your RV.

One of the easiest ways to do this is to obtain a language program on CD and simply listen on your dash CD player. Of course the most ideal way to do this is while you are parked in a campground, but you can follow the process while you are driving.

Then there is language software. One of the best tools for learning a new language is the Rosetta Stone software program. There are at least thirty language programs available with the approach being interactive and fun. Lessons are offered through a progression of step-by-step lessons.

If you have online connectivity, there are website that offer courses. *Word2word.com* offers links to courses in most languages with many free tutorials. *Sanishromance.com* also provides resources to learn Spanish for free.

Museums Online

Many museums offer an online presence through their respective links. You can gather an array of exhibits and collections including classic art and architecture.

If you log onto The Museum of Online Museums (*coudal.com/moom.php*) you'll find many links to brick and mortar museums.

VLMP (*vlmp.icom.museum*) is a worldwide directory of online museums that are organized by country.

Museumstuff.com boasts a staggering variety of educational links along with interactive virtual exhibits.

Museums In Person

The beauty of owning an RV is that you can travel to a wonderful location to enjoy both the beauty of nature and the cultural offerings available.

I highly recommend a visit to the Georgia O'Keefe Museum (*okeeffemuseum.org*) in Santa Fe, New Mexico. Aside from devoted itself to the artistic legacy of Georgia O'Keefe, it is committed to the study and interpretation of American modernism. In addition, there are at least twelve campgrounds in the area offering all levels of amenities. In some locations, you can even leave the rig and take public transportation.

Another very interesting location to visit is New Orleans. The truly historic nature of the area is the basis for a large variety of museums. Included here are:

- Mardi Gras Museums
- Religious Museums
- New Orleans Jazz National Historic Park
- African American Museum
- Contemporary Arts Center
- Herman Grima House
- Nature Museums

Log onto *neworleansmuseums.com* for a detailed list of museums.

There are a variety of city campgrounds in the area, some of which offer the convenience of public transportation directly from the premises. I've done that a number of times and greatly appreciate not having to drive in the city. You can check out Jude Travel Park (*judetravelpark.com*), The New Orleans RV Campground (*neworleanscampground.com*), and The French Quarter RV Resort (*fqrv.com*). All of these camps offer a variety of amenities.

If you visit the Boston, MA area, be certain to visit the Museum of Fine Arts (*mfa.org*), The Museum of Science, (*mos.org*), The USS Constitution (*ussconstitutionmuseum.org*), and The Children's Museum (*boston kids.org*). The latter is particularly helpful if you have grandchildren with you. Normandy Farms Campground (*normandyfarms.com*) is quite close and transportation is available into the city. They also offer a wide variety of recreational activities right at the campground including indoor swimming pools and a snack bar.

Libraries Online

If you have a thirst for knowledge, there is a wealth of information available through online library resources. Also, if you are matriculating at an online college, you can do your research through these online mechanisms. For example, it is easy to read book reviews, explore literary criticism, read scholarly journals, and search newspaper archives.

Similarly, it is easy to visit online reference desks to gain information, and you can search databases of law and medical libraries.

A great place to start is *libraryspot.com*. The site is a free virtual library resource center for anyone doing research on the web. The Reading Room link allows you to check out book reviews, journals, and newspapers. You can also search a large variety of libraries listed by state.

The Internet Public Library (*ipl.org*) is basically a public Internet Library. It features authoritative collections, information assistance, and a variety of other library services including an online collection of newspapers from around the world.

You can also access the Yahoo Reference Library site (*dir.yahoo.com/Reference/Libraries/*) if you are looking for a huge variety of libraries that are listed by individual categories.

Great Courses (*thegreatcourses.com***)**

This company offers a wide variety of courses on DVD and CD presented by a variety of professors. They have put together over two hundred courses for lifelong learners. The best part is, there is no homework or exams. Their catalogue is very thorough and descriptive. Course categories include science and mathematics, art and music, literature and English language, music, philosophy, religion, and history.

I've perused their faculty and most have Doctorate or medical degrees with a great amount of teaching experience.

SeniorNet (*seniornet.org*)

Assuming that have you that all-important Internet Connectivity while on the road, SeniorNet can be a very good learning source. They now offer a full catalog of facilitated online courses on a broad range of topics including computers, digital photography, genealogy, health, personal finance, history, languages, writing, literature and more.

Most courses are offered over a six-week period. Students do interact with instructors and other students. As a member of SeniorNet you pay only sixty-nine dollars per course. They do offer a pioneering Classical Latin Course that is very popular.

AARP (*aarp.org*)

The AARP website is quite informative offering a variety of learning experiences. The Topics in the "Learning and Technology" link will take you to a plethora of online course offerings. There are courses available in finance, literature, art, health and well-being, technology and more. Most of the offerings are free of charge.

CHAPTER 12: KEEPING IN SHAPE ON THE ROAD

Here's an interesting bit of information. Recent reports indicate that people over the age of fifty are the fastest-growing segment of the fitness population. Because we are living longer, more healthier lives these days, here is a major reason behind this trend: Most Baby Boomers don't want to feel "old" as they grow older. So, more of an emphasis is being placed on the quality of life and specifically on physical health – making it a top priority.

I am obsessed about keeping in good physical condition. The results of my most recent physical examination indicate that I continue to be in excellent health for my age (sixty-two). I follow a steadfast routine of exercise when at home or on the road. The specific benefits that I've noticed include increased endurance, better balance, and constant flexibility of my muscles.

Certainly, the most important first step is to check with your doctor before commencing any new physical activity. If exercising causes you to experience excessive shortness of breath, light-headedness, or difficulty with balance, stop and consult your doctor.

When you are on the road in your RV, your exercise routine may change dramatically, depending on weather conditions, and where you camp. I've found that campground gyms are a rarity. So, what are your choices?

Swimming

If you are camping in warm weather, the campground pool should be readily available. If you are looking for a low impact exercise, support by a natural resistance, aquatic exercise may be for you. In addition, many campgrounds do indeed offer water aerobics classes. Types of activities may involve jogging, stretching, and the use of weights.

Additionally, when searching out RV parks, check your directory carefully and try to locate a camp that has an indoor pool. When traveling around the country, I often times camp at the Amarillo RV Ranch in Amarillo, Texas or the Rockwell RV Park in Oklahoma City, Oklahoma because of this convenient amenity.

Walking, Speed Walking, Running

I've found that at the end of a long day on the road in my RV, there is nothing more refreshing than a speed walk. As I travel around the country, I have not come across one campground where

I cannot plot out a walking path. I've consulted with campground personnel numbers of times on this matter. Normally, my walks last thirty minutes. That is in line with many recommendations from medical experts, who suggest three thirty-minute walks a week at a brisk pace may be all that you need.

Bicycling

According to the National Sporting Goods Association, retirees and near retirees now account for twenty percent of all those over the age of seven who rode a bike at least six times a year. That figure is up thirteen percent from a decade ago. The appeal of cycling is most pronounced among the youngest boomers who, as I said earlier, are embracing a healthy lifestyle.

My wife and I have been biking for at least twenty years. Much of that biking involves carrying our bike with us either on the back of the RV or inside of the tow vehicle. You'll notice that I used the word "bike." We have been a tandem couple since 1995. These days we carry a folding Bike Friday (*bikefriday.com*) tandem with us that conveniently stores in the back of our Honda CRV. It takes about ninety seconds to take out the bike, unfold it, and get ready to ride. We usually find a plethora of paths or streets to bike directly from our campgrounds.

Bike Friday and Dahon (*dahon.com*) sell a variety of single folding bikes that are even easier to transport. In fact, most of those will easily fit in an external storage compartment on your RV.

There are a large number of bike trail publications available. A good source is *Amazon.com*. You can do a specific search for the area of your interest. The *Best Bike Paths of New England* and the *Best Bike Paths of the Southwest* by Wendy Williams are good choices. Additionally, you can obtain further information from the National Park Service (*nps.gov*) or at individual State Parks. Log onto *pedaling.com*, a site that offers new route information for and by the biking community with an excellent search mechanism. You will be able to set your own parameters for distance, steepness of grade, and surrounding environment.

Hiking

I am constantly reminded of our many camping trips over the last forty years, which included my mother-in-law. When she was sixty-three, she climbed a three thousand foot trail on Mt. Monadnock in New Hampshire. At the time we were camping in the beautiful State Park near the mountain. She continued to hike until she was eighty years old.

My experience has shown that hiking has three distinct advantages:

1. Exercise
2. Learning
3. Creating good karma

My wife and I feel so exhilarated within the hiking environment, that we are able to carry that feeling forward throughout the rest of our daily activities.

I've found that most campground offices have hiking information available to patrons. You can also obtain trail maps at most visitor centers or chambers of commerce.

The Falcon Guides (*falcon.com*) series is an excellent source for hiking locations around the country. The guides are easy to understand and quite descriptive.

Exercising In and Around the RV

If you do not have available time to engage in the aforementioned activities, perhaps keeping fit around the campsite is a useful alternative.

Many RVers prefer to exercise within the confines of the RV. If that is your choice, it is important that you pay special attention to floor plans when you are looking to purchase a rig. You will need to have space to exercise, even if the exercises are of a stationary nature.

RESISTANCE BAND EXERCISES

Resistance band exercises are widely used by both for general strength and conditioning and rehabilitation or injury prevention. They help to condition your cardiovascular system as well as specific muscle groups. Since resistance tubing is so compact and lightweight, it is a natural for use on the road in your RV. You can actually store them in a Ziploc bag. Examples of resistance band exercises include:

- resistance band squats
- resistance band bent over rows
- chest presses
- diagonal woodchips (pulls)
- tricep extensions
- lateral rows with the band

Resistance bands are available at Amazon (*amazon.com*), and most major sporting goods retailers.

YOGA

Many experts say Yoga is actually considered a form of exercise. That is, it is an excellent form of exercise for the mind and spirit. In terms of physical exercise, many of the poses associated with yoga require great physical flexibility. Stretching of muscles is required, which in turn increases your overall range of motion and makes you less vulnerable to injury. Many yoga routines will boost endurance and stamina.

Strength and power play individual roles to achieve a perfect balance in every part of the body. After each stimulating exercise, a sense of rejuvenation follows. If you are interested in Yoga on the road you will need to take a mat with you in the RV.

"WII – FIT"

Here's a unique idea. If you have the space in your RV, and you are into technology, why not buy a Wii Gaming Console by Nintendo. As I discuss in the next chapter, Wii is a whole body interactive experience. It offers more than forty physical activities including yoga, fitness training, balance games and aerobics. All of the fitness activities are performed on the Wii Balance Board, which is a peripheral to the gaming console. The Wii Balance Board is able to read a user's real-life movements and bring them to life on the TV screen. Your motions are tracked on the screen. Your performance is also measured by the gaming console, allowing you to gauge your progress as you pursue your fitness goals. Remember, only a small storage space is needed for Wii components.

OTHER SIMPLE SUGGESTIONS

Assuming that you are traveling in an RV that has some reasonable outside storage, there are some additional exercise items that you can take along.

I've seen a great number of over fifty-five campers that do enjoy roller blading. Needless to say, make sure that you are well padded.

You can always find space to carry a jump rope and a frisbee. Additionally, if you have a DVD player, bring along an exercise DVD. Those exercises do not require a great deal of space and you will get a good workout.

Finally, there are a variety of no excuse exercises that anyone can do in the RV. Those include:

- push-ups
- leg lifts
- crunches

- tummy tucks
- neck rolls

CHAPTER 13: ENTERTAINMENT IN THE RV

After forty years of RVing, I've found few things more satisfying than being digitally entertained in the rig after a long hard day on the road. After the routine tasks of hooking-up, and opening the slides, I just love put a DVD in the player, turn on the surround sound system along with the flat panel, and just relax. I may even connect a gaming console.

The Digital Age

Fortunately for the RVer, the digital age has made things more comfortable. That is, much of the entertainment technology has become smaller. As every RV owner knows, space in the rig can be at a premium. So, if we plan things right we can do more with less storage space.

If you have a reasonably new RV, chances are that you may have a built-in TV, and DVD player. If you do not have the aforementioned technology, there is a solution to save space and expense.

If you currently own a laptop computer, it can function as a TV (see the paragraph below on Apple TV), CD player, music library storage, DVD player, a DVD recorder, an extensive photo album (with photo editing capabilities assuming you have the appropriate software installed), and a movie player (allowing you to download movies, or play movies stored).

By the way, if you do not already have one, you may want to consider the purchase of an iPod (or similar MP3 player). In addition to be able to carry around a portable music library and photo library, it can act as a backup drive for the laptop from which you can download all sorts of fun things including free lectures from the all new Apple iTunes University.

In addition to saving space in your RV, you will be able to conserve energy by not having as many components plugged in. By using your laptop in this manner, it becomes a digital hub. You will have to engage in some thoughtful planning in an effort to decide what you really want to do. Then you would move forward and select equipment that will best fit your needs. As previously mentioned, you do have the potential of saving a great deal of space.

Digital Television

If you are a veteran RVer you are familiar with the old Bat Wing Antenna that came with most RV's of years past. You were used to watching that fuzzy reception, accompanied by poor sound, interference and limited channel reception.

Nowadays, you do have a variety of options available. Times have changed. Clearer reception, better sound and a large variety of channels are available with a digital HD receiver.

Many High Definition come with a built-in digital tuner and HDMI digital inputs. And you may even find a PC input so you can use the TV as a computer monitor.

The obvious choices for reception are the standard TV antenna, cable hook-up, or satellite dish. The simplest satellite antennas are those that are stationary or of a portable nature. For more discussion on satellite antennas see Chapter 9. If you do not have a dish, then you are limited to your standard TV antenna or a cable connection within the campground, if that service is available.

Apple TV *(apple.com)*

Apple TV is another media gadget from the "gadget innovators" at Apple Computer. It basically turns your living room into an on-demand movie theatre by allowing you to rent movies using your remote control and your wide screen TV. And, you do not need a computer! You will need a broadband connection for the quickest downloading. If you have a satellite dish with Internet connectivity, you should be fine.

Another great feature of Apple TV that is very compatible with the RV lifestyle is the fact that you only need a space that is 8"X8" and 1" thick. Connectivity is wireless. You can browse the iTunes store then purchase and download your favorite movies, commercial free TV shows, and music.

Gaming Consoles

There are a variety of gaming consoles on the market that can easily adapt to the RV lifestyle. As previously discussed, one of the most popular choices at the time of this writing is Wii. Wii is a social gaming experience for the whole family. It is actually a great campground activity as you can get together with friends and engage in an interactive experience.

One of the unique features of Wii is that users can play with their whole bodies as opposed to merely operating a control pad. It comes with a group of sports games including tennis, golf, bowling and baseball. Additional games can be purchased separately. The remote control essentially translates body motion and translates it to the screen.

DVD Board Games

For those of you who love board games a new visual element has been added in the form of an interactive DVD format.

These games are a great way to entertain the family. You are surrounded by the game board while taking cues from the TV screen. The difficult part here is deciding which game to play. You can choose from Monopoly, chess, backgammon, Mastermind, trivia games, and many more.

Digital Scrapbooking

If you have software such as Adobe Photoshop and you have online connectivity, making a digital scrapbook is easy. After you create your pages you can upload them to great websites such as Flickr (*flickr.com*), or iStockphoto (*istockphoto.com*), or Revver (*revver.com*). These sites allow you share photos and video, and even engage in some sales.

Satellite Radio

As of this writing there are about 8 million people who subscribe to satellite radio. Just in case you did not know, satellite radio creates the broadcasting of static-free radio from digital signals that are sent from space through satellites. There are over one-hundred satellite radio stations that broadcast any kind of programming one could think of, all without commercial interruption. Chances are that your favorite national radio host will show up on a satellite channel along with a variety of entertainment services offered by the service providers. You do need to subscribe. XM Satellite Radio and Sirius are the two major providers. Monthly rates begin at about twelve dollars and a receiver is required.

In terms of weather you should get a satellite radio system, it is really a simple decision. I feel that it is something you must have. If you are an active RVer and are on the road a great deal of the time you are guaranteed coast-to-coast reception.

MP3 Players

An MP3 player is a device that plays audio digital audio and video files. The most popular mp3 player is the Apple iPod. These players allow you to carry along in your RV thousands of pictures, songs, and videos. For example, the 80GB or 160GB iPod has up to forty hours of battery life and lets you enjoy 40,000 songs or up to two hundred hours of video, wherever you go.

Kindle: A Wireless Reader From Amazon

Kindle is a portable wireless reading device that allows you to download books, blogs, magazines, and newspapers. It is perfect for limited RV storage space. You can adjust text size. It comes with a built-in dictionary, and it has long battery life. The display offers a sharp, high-resolution screen. Also, it is very lightweight.

More than 160, 000 books are available and you can store over two hundred titles on Kindle. The average cost for a book download is about ten dollars. No monthly fees are charged for the service.

CHAPTER 14: ORGANIZATIONS THAT SUPPORT YOUR RV RETIREMENT LIFESTYLE

There are a number of organizations that are made up of people just like you, which offer a plethora of benefits to make your retirement lifestyle more comfortable and accommodating. These organizations may offer discounts on goods and services to its members. You will also find an abundance of information exchanges that will make your travels less stressful.

The following are some examples of the most popular clubs.

Good Sam Club (*goodsamclub.com)*

The Good Sam has about 1 million members these days. Their goal is to make RVing more enjoyable while meeting responsibilities to the environment.

Some of the benefits include:

- member only website which provides access to member forums – where you can post travel tips, share road experiences and receive helpful advice
- enrollment in SamAlert which tracks National Highway Traffic Administration recall information

- presentation of product reviews
- information about the latest legislation relating to the rights of RVers
- money saving discounts on gas, RV Parks, camping publications and road service
- mail forwarding service

It should be noted that their recently redesigned website includes a Travel Tools section which places comprehensive travel information at your fingertips. This feature works in conjunction with Trailer Life Directory

(*trailerlifedirectory.com*).

The site utilizes truck-mapping software that is an excellent tool for RVers. Its updated trip-routing feature includes information about bridge and tunnel restrictions, towing laws, campground ratings, attractions, and upcoming events.

Family Motor Coach Association (*fmca.com*)

I've been a member of this club for twenty-five years. It is primarily made up of members who are motorhome owners. At the time of this writing there are about 120,000 active member families. However, I've not specifically owned motorcoaches during the last forty years and have continued to maintain my membership. That is mainly because of the useful information I receive from their magazines and the website. That information includes articles on travel destinations, great recipes, industry trends, and the latest technology.

Additional membership benefits include:

- mail forwarding
- free trip routing
- emergency road service
- emergency driver availability
- free insurance
- educational programs
- gas and campground discounts
- medical evacuation
- area rallies and conventions
- financial services
- insurance

RV.NET

RV.NET is a network of RV sites that are dedicated to serving enthusiasts of the open road. They offer a forum link, an RV blog, and an online campground directory database.

A check of the forum link indicates discussions on a wide variety of topics, from what type of RV to select, to various reflections on the RV lifestyle. I find it very useful to read other opinions on RV experiences with pets, cooking issues, health difficulties on the road, and RV rallies. At the time of this writing there were also a plethora of discussions on technical resources.

The campground database allows you to search a variety of directories and also features a driving directions link. You can check on ratings of the campgrounds as well.

Anther very useful link is the RV Reviews. Here you will be able to read about reviews of RVs and related RV products.

Escapees RV Club (*escapees.com*)

This club offers a variety of basic-to-advanced classes, seminars, and workshops that are taught by RV experts who have had a great deal of experience in their fields of expertise.

Their Boot Camp Classes consist of essential information about safety and the nuts and bolts of RVing.

The RVing Forums are chock full of discussions on such topics as getting started in the RV lifestyle, the full-time RV lifestyle, technical tips and tricks, budgeting, volunteering adventures, and destination choices.

Other benefits of this club include mail forwarding, a travel guide, Escapees Care (provides professional assistance to Rvers who live in their RV while recovering from illness or injury), an advocacy group, and a magazine.

Family Campers & Rvers *(fcrv.org)*

Some of the goals of FCRV include:

- encouraging people to participate in recreational activities which protect and conserve and defend our natural resources
- promoting physical fitness, sound camping, and an appreciation of nature
- continuing education and charitable purposes

This club engages in many types of humanitarian activities on the national, regional, and state levels. They attempt to promote fun, friendship, and fellowship among RVers.

Activities involve a wildlife refuge program, disaster awareness training, and a conservation program designed to help local chapters of the club to correct environmental problems in their own areas.

Loners on Wheels (*lonersonwheels.com***)**

The membership of this club consists of single men and women who enjoy traveling, camping, RV caravanning, and in general, the lifestyle of single people. The basic premise of the club is to offer companionship and support for the membership, with an emphasis on sharing interests. But, they insist that matchmaking is not a goal. They do publish a monthly newsletter.

So, you will find a schedule of monthly campouts, caravans, and rallies on tap. At the time of this writing, the location of most events is in the Southwest.

The headquarters and gathering place of the club is a sixty-five acre RV Park in Deming, New Mexico.

RVing Women (*rvingwomen.org***)**

The membership of this club is made up of a diverse group of women across the US and Canada who enjoy RVing and love to travel.

A network of support and friendship is offered by the membership. Rving Women links you to members who can offer information, suggest places to see, things to do, and provide assistance when needed. There is also access available to technical and general information related to RVing.

Some of the current goals of the club include:

- assisting with the long-term legal and financial health of RVing women
- addressing the changing social, recreational, and educational needs of women RVers
- increasing opportunities for members to participate in leadership and other volunteer experiences

Campground Discount & Membership Clubs

For the most part, the following clubs focus on campground discounts along with other services. These RV clubs can help reduce expenses if you are on a budget. Be certain to evaluate the cost of membership to see if you can save some money over the long haul and if the campgrounds are located in areas that interest you.

- Happy Campers (*happycampers.org)*
- Passport America (*passportamerica.com*)
- Recreation USA (*campingandcampgrounds.com)*
- Thousand Trails (*thousandtrails.com*)
- Resort Parks International (*resortparks.com*)
- Resorts of Distinction *(resortsofdistinction.com*)
- Camp Club USA (*campclubusa.com*)

CHAPTER 15: SUGGESTED DESTINATIONS

Are you still thinking of your RV as a tool to support and accommodate your retirement lifestyle? After forty years of Rving, I've learned that my coach is a great way to implement that all-important retirement plan.

In my first book, *The New Professional Person's Retirement Lifestyle,* I discuss in detail how to create such a plan with valid goals, all in the spirit of reinventing and rediscovering yourself. So, if you've decided that you would like to travel in your RV for purposes of learning about our beautiful country, pursuing a new hobby, researching genealogy, or even sightseeing, you've got the open road awaiting.

Here are some varied suggestions for destinations.

Charleston, South Carolina (*charlestoncvb.com*)

There is much to do in this Southern city. Historic landmarks, outstanding architecture, fine art, and modern attractions beckon you.

Locals claim that Charleston is the culture capital of the South. Visitors can tour 18 century homes and plantations; parks, museums and historic churches; and a large and impressive city market. Art lovers will want to visit one the many city art galleries. Here are some great things to do in Charleston.

- Gibbes Museum of Art – opened in 1905
- Charles Town Landing State Historic Site – located where colonists established the area's first European Settlement
- Classic Carriage Tour – Tour the city in a horse drawn carriage
- Drayton Hall – National Trust historic site
- South Carolina Aquarium – The structure extends our over Charleston Harbor.
- Charleston Museum – historical materials from the earliest settlements
- Fort Sumter National Monument – site where the Civil War began
- Lowcountry Ghost Walk – a popular tour filled with ghostly legends
- Cypress Gardens – includes eighty acres of swamp that can be viewed from flat-bottomed boats.
- Gibbes Museum of Art – over 10,000 pieces of art are featured.

Ocala National Forest, Ocala Florida

This is the second largest National Forest in Florida and it is the southernmost national forest in America. Here, you can camp in a safe environment within bear and gator country. During the winter the temperatures average around 70 degrees. If you travel an hour away, you will find yourself in world-class attractions. The natural beauty here is pristine. There are nineteen campgrounds three of which offer large spring-fed swimming holes that average 72 degrees year-round.

The Ocala springs are not just for swimming. Bring your canoe or kayak and head downstream. There is a canoe trail that runs seven miles through a cypress forest.

Warm days in late winter or early spring can yield alligators, some measuring up to twelve feet in length.

The St. Johns River borders that forest in the east. The river is one of the bass-fishing treasures of the country. You can even try your hand at trapping blue crabs.

A canoe or boat trip up the Silver River will present you with a view of exotic animals including a variety of monkeys.

For a different view of the forest you can hike one of the one hundred miles of trails. The Florida National Scenic Trail comes to mind with its sixty-five miles of beauty. You can stroll through mixed cabbage palms and cypress swamps without getting your feet wet.

The Ocala National Forest also offers twenty-two miles of mountain bike trails with open sand track.

Campgrounds in the National Forest offer a variety of amenities. So, you find sites that are primitive along with those that offer paved roads and pads, along with running water for filling your tank and hot showers with flush toilets. None of the forest camps offer hookups but there are private campgrounds in the area.

Joshua Tree National Park, California (*nps.gov/jotr*)

This is a place where you can get away from it all. It is located where the Mojave and Colorado deserts merge. You could say it is a location of many attractions: rock climbing, trails for hiking and exploring, dirt roads for mountain biking, and an abundance of wild flowers come Spring.

The preserve includes 794,000 acres located just two hours from Pomona. You'll find hundred of plant species, two hundred forty varieties of birds, forty species of reptiles, and forty-one mammal species.

The campground is open year-round and sites are available on a first-come first-served basis with no hookups offered.

Hikers and walkers will want to explore the trails near the campground and beyond. The park boasts one hundred ninety-one miles of trails, some with expansive vistas. In fact, from the summit you will see the jagged peaks of the San Jacinto Mountains.

If you take a driving tour through Joshua Tree you will be quite impressed with the mountain views of Eagle, Coxcomb, Pinto, Hexie, and Cottonwood Mountains.

Joshua Trees are slow-growing yucca plants. Full-grown trees provide nesting places for a variety of birds including owls and woodpeckers.

From White Tank Campground, you can travel about twenty miles to the 5,195-foot view at Keys View, along with the 11,000 foot view of the San Jacinto range. To the south, the fabulous view of the Salton Sea awaits you.

Be sure to head north to the Hidden Valley/Barker Damn area and, bring your camera.

A Glimpse at Paradise: Welcome to Belize

Can you imagine driving your RV to a tropical country? Picture yourself horseback riding through a mahogany jungle or swimming around coral reefs.

Belize is just south of Mexico's Yucatan Peninsula. It has wonderful beaches and what the country says is the largest barrier reef in the world.

There are only two roads into Belize: one from Mexico and one from Guatemala. The country contains numerous Mayan ruins. The pyramid at Caracol is the tallest man-made structure in the country.

If you have a motorhome you need not be worried about driving in Belize. Roads are paved, most with two wide lanes. There are only four main roads around the country, so it is hard to get lost.

There are a great many jungle hikes near San Ignacio on the western highway near Guatemala. You can even rent horses to take in the beauty of the tropical broadleaf forest where you'll see orchids, mahogany white monkeys and macaws.

Belize has more formal campsites than most of Central America. Still there are not many available. Often times, campers pay additional charges for electric hookups at the campsite. There are many commercial establishments that will allow you to boondock (park in their lot). Always be certain to ask for permission.

More than one third of Belize consists of nature preserves, parks, and sanctuaries. There are a variety of animal including a baboon refuge.

The best time to visit Belize is between November and April. During this time, you may avoid the rainy season and the resulting unpaved wet roads that become difficult to navigate.

If you are the adventurous sort, Belize offers history, culture, beaches, and beautiful jungles. And, the local residents will make you feel very welcome.

The Alamo, San Antonio, Texas (*thealamo.org*)

Do you remember the story behind the Alamo? To refresh your memory, in 1836 one hundred eighty-nine Texans stood tall against the Mexican Army. When the Alamo finally fell, its defenders became American legends. The inspirational "Remember the Alamo!" has been repeated over and over through the years. The cry is a haunting reminder of a time when men valued freedom more than life.

If you visit The Alamo you will find campgrounds that provide easy access to the downtown area including the availability of public transportation. It is helpful to know that the Alamo is a city attraction, and is surrounded by a number of hotels and a post office.

A striking feature inside the shrine is the large number of states and nations represented in the defense of a young Texas. One entire room is devoted to Davy Crockett, the frontiersman who became a defender of the Alamo.

Another interesting thing to do while you are in San Antonio is to walk the River Walk with its accompanying cobblestone walkways. You'll pass through an assortment of quaint shops, elegant boutiques and wonderful restaurants right alongside of the San Antonio River that flows throughout the city.

Fairbanks, Alaska – Interesting Stops

If you are planning to take that long awaited RV trip to Alaska on the Alaska Highway, wonderful attractions await you. Make certain that you explore The *Milepost Magazine*. The contents will help you identify the fun, unusual, rewarding, educational and cultural activities and attractions. Some of the major attractions include:

- Anchorage
- Dawson City
- Fairbanks
- Glaciers
- Inside Passage
- Mount McKinley

Here are several suggested places to visit near Fairbanks:

At the Alyeska Trans-Alaska Pipeline viewing station you can stand underneath the massive supports and actually touch the pipeline. As the pipeline crosses the state, it traverses three mountain ranges and makes thirty-four river crossings. The viewing station is eight miles north of Fairbanks and ample RV parking is available.

The University of Alaska Museum of the North features 2000 years of Alaskan native art including ancient ivory carvings and woven Aleut grass baskets. Other exhibits showcase the effect of world cultures upon Alaskan history including objects representing the influence of early colonization. There is a display of Japanese memorabilia from World War II that reminds visitors of the Japanese invasion of the Aleutian Islands and the difficulties American forces endured.

The Eilson Air Force Base is located twenty-three miles south of Fairbanks. Tours are about ninety minutes in length. On the tour you'll see a partially submerged WB-29 aircraft, and possibly even F-16 fighters speed down the airstrip. You will also visualize what life is like on the 63,000-acre facility. Base residents even have their own ski slope and lodge. A stop on the tour includes a training hangar where you can look at an F-16.

Campgrounds in the vicinity include Chena Marina RV Park (*chinarvpark.com*) with breakfast, wi-fi and full hookups. River's Edge RV Park (*riversedge.net*) is located alongside the Chena River.

Five Very Popular National Parks

GREAT SMOKY MOUNTAINS NATIONAL PARK (*nps.gov/grsm*)

U.S Route 441 climbs up and over the park's midsection and affords sweeping views of waterfalls, rocky pinnacles, and ridge tops. Enjoy a drive to historic mills and old Appalachia. There are 800 miles of horse and foot trails. The drive has a variety of upgrades and hairpin turns, but most big rigs can handle it. Clingmans Dome abounds with animals and the fishing can be great. There are ten campgrounds and none offer hookups.

GRAND CANYON NATIONAL PARK (nps.gov/grca)

A park ranger at Grand Canyon National Park once stated that he envied anybody's first view of the canyon.

I can clearly recall how awestruck I was back in 1970 when my wife and I first visited the area. Our camping vehicle was a Dodge van and we simply slept in the back of that panel van. As we had no personal facilities, it was simply a situation of being as one with nature surrounded by all of that astounding beauty of the one-mile deep canyon.

If you have nerves of steel, you can ride a mule down a dizzying South Rim Trail. Or you can hike from rim to rim.

Since most people visit the South Rim, make certain that you reserve a campsite at Mather Campground way in advance. The same rule of thumb applies to the mule rides. The North Rim receives only one-tenth of the park's visitors, which is rather unfortunate because it does have breathtaking vistas.

YELLOWSTONE NATIONAL PARK (nps.gov/yell)

Yellowstone has 10,000 geysers and hot springs. Steamboat is the world's tallest sometimes reaching three hundred feet. Old Faithful is not so high, but is very predictable. Incredible vistas of lakes, waterfalls, bubbling mud pots, and vales await you.

You will also find a large variety of wildlife including grizzly bears, wolves, bison and elk.

Activities include horseback riding, fishing, hiking, boating, and bicycling.

Twelve of Yellowstone's campgrounds accept Rvs and five take reservations. In fact, some even have big-rig sites. Fishing Bridge is the only park with hookups.

OLYMPIC NATIONAL PARK (nps.gov/olym)

This park encompasses Pacific Ocean beaches, rain forest valleys, glacier-capped peaks, and a stunning variety of plants and animals. The heart of this park is the wilderness. It is a refuge for both humans and creatures.

Drive to the mile-high treeline and you will be astounded by the panoramic views of the Olympic Mountains and the Strait of Juan de Fuca far below. You can walk along the shoreline of Lake crescent and see live glaciers still at work on the peaks. The Hoh Rain Forest is one of the most beautiful in the Pacific Northwest. There are nearly a million acres that take you through beach, forest and mountains.

The park has sixteen campgrounds. None of those have hookups. Some are closed during the winter. There are a couple of private RV resorts along the way. Sol Duc Hot Springs and Lob Cabin do have hookups.

Central Oregon Coast

The Pacific Coast Scenic Byway (U.S. Highway 101) hugs the coast and affords you easy access to area beaches, lighthouses, old-growth forests and miles of hiking trails.

If you like to bike, trails abound. You will experience some of the most invigorating sights around as you wind your way along the coastline truly enjoying nature. People from around the world enjoy the Oregon Coast Bike Route. It travels for 370 miles along Highway 101 and will take you six to eight days to travel the entire length.

The central coast is a diverse region that includes Seal Rock, the southern region of towering cliffs and the coastal rain forest between Yachats and Florence.

Campgrounds in the area are plentiful with four of the most popular Oregon State Parks in the area. In addition, there are many county, private and national forest campgrounds. You can easily select one campground and make it your base to explore the area. During the summer months, campsites in the State Parks are very much in demand, so be certain to make a reservation.

Whale watching is also a very popular activity on the Oregon coast. Twelve thousand whales migrate to the warm Mexican waters beginning in late November.

Sea Lion Caves, south of Heceta Head, is the year-round home to a colony of Steller sea lions. The sea lions leave the caves to bask on the sunny rock cliffs where they breed.

Cost Effective Destination Cities

If you do your research, you'll find that certain city-based campgrounds in interesting destinations are close to many sightseeing attractions. You may also find that public transportation is readily available nearby. So, why take the motor vehicle along when you can save fuel and do your part for environmental issues?

Independence, Missouri has a full –service campground within walking distance to many attractions. Campus RV Park is close to the Independence and Kansas City areas.

In New Orleans, the Big Easy KOA is close to the French Quarter and Bourbon Street. In fact, they do offer a shuttle right in to the city. Or, the city bus is right nearby.

We have also found that Los Campos RV Resort is very convenient to beautiful Santa Fe, New Mexico. It is only four miles to downtown and there is public bus service available.

Be certain to check city campgrounds in your RV directory to verify a city park location if you would rather not drive.

WEBSITE DIRECTORY

BOONDOCKING

boondocking.org – public database of boondocking locations

boondockingguide.com – a non-commercial guide

rvtravel.com/blog/boondocking – boondocking blog

your-rv-lifestyle.com/boondocking.html – boondocking tips

DESTINATIONS

your-rv-lifestyle.com/places-to-rv

/www.two-lane.com/lifestyle

nps.gov – all National Park information

charlestoncvb.com – info on Charleston, S.C.

thealamo.org – visitors guide to The Alamo

belize-guide.info – a comprehensive guide to Belize

travelalaska.com – Alaska Division of Tourism

lovetheoutdoors.com/camping – a listing of state tourism websites

DISTANCE LEARNING

uopxonline.com – University of Phoenix Online

uclaextension.edu – UCLA extension program

dir.yahoo.com/Education/Distance_Learning – Yahoo Distance Learning

petersons.com/distancelearning/ - Peterson's continuing education

distancelearn.about.com/ – a listing of online classes from about.com

FULLTIMING

fulltiming-america.com – helpful links for fulltimers

your-rv-lifestyle.com/fulltiming.html – general advice

trailerlife.com/fulltiming – helpful links offered by the RV magazine

fulltimerver.com – news and information

rv-links.com/fuilltiming – latest fulltiming news

HOBBIES AND INTERESTS

antiqueresources.com – timely discussions on antiques

antiquesandhearts.com – online events newspaper

freedigitalscrapbooking.com – offers digital freebies

digitalscrapbookplace.com – creative ideas for scrapbooks

ghostranch.org – beautiful surroundings along with diverse courses

folkschool.org – situated in the mountains of North Carolina

roadsideamerica.com – offbeat cultural tourist attractions

advrider.com/forums/ - a forum for bikes and riders

hamradio-online.com – ham radio blog

INTERNET ACCESS IN THE RV

rvnetworking.com

dustyfoot.com

internetanywhere.us

verizonwireless.com

wireless.att.com

internetbycellphone.com

t-mobile.com

sprint.com

RENTALS

cruiseamericarv.com/rv_rentals/costs/default.asp domestic

elmonterv.com/ domestic

motorhomesworldwide.com/motorhome/index.shtml worldwide

motorhomerentals.com/ wordwide

RV LIFESTYLE:

www.your-rv-lifestyle.com/your-rv-lifestyle.html

your-rv-lifestyle.com/

RV CLUBS

goodsamclub.com – the nation's largest club

fmca.com – club for motorcoach owners

lonersonwheels.com – membership limited to single campers and travelers; not a matchmaking service

naarva.com – National African American Rvers Association

rvingwomen.org – women who love to travel

fcrv.org – Family Camper & Rvers

escapees.com – features classes in RVing

gonct.org – National Camping Travelers – a Masonic club

RV COMMUNITIES

retirenet.com/types/rv/

bestretirementspots.com/RV.htm

suncommunities.com/corporate/

loopnet.com/

RV FORUMS

rv.net – largest participation of all forums

rvforum.net – popular with retirees

rvtravel.com - features a variety of travel blogs

rvlivin.com – includes forums, classifieds, and RV related news

myrvspace.com

escapees.infopop.cc – general RV discussion forum

RV PURCHASE

rvtraderonline.com – new and used prices

Craigslist – craigslist.org – a major site for bargains

Ebay.com – bid on your RV dream

nadaguides.com – authoritative source for checking book values
fabuloustravel.com/ - advice on how and when to buy an RV

RV TOURS AND RALLIES

creativeworldtravel.com – Creative World RV Rallies
fantasytoursrv.com – guided rv tours

khulsey.com/rv – calendar of RV rallies

adventurecaravans.com – guided tours offered in the U.S., Canada and Mexico

yankeervtours.com – unique escorted tours in the U.S. and Canada

VOLUNTEERING ON THE ROAD

nps.gov – National Park Service

www.fs.fed.us/fsjobs/jobs_volunteers.shtm - US Forest Service

volunteer.gov/gov – public sector volunteer opportunities

happyvagabonds.com – state park volunteers

orn.usace.army.mil/volunteer/ - Army Corps of Engineers

blm.gov/volunteer/ - US Department of the Interior

habitat.org – Habitat For Humanity has RV Care-A-Vanner program

literacyvolunteers.org – Literacy Volunteers of America

peacecorps.gov – Peace Corps

seniorcorps.org – includes Foster Grandparent Program
servenet.org – expansive list of volunteer opportunities

volunteermatch.org – database of opportunities that can be searched by zip code

netaid.org – virtual volunteering opportunites

WORKAMPING

nps.gov/personnel – careers opportunities with the NPS

www.fs.fed.us/fsjobs – temporary employment with the Forrest Service

yellowstonejobs.com – jobs at Yellowstone Park

rvhometown.com/HTML/SYRVL/about_SYRVL.htm

workamper.com - a variety of resources related to workamping

coolworks.com - assistance in finding seasonal jobs

seasonaemployment.com - search seasonal jobs by state

myprimeyears.com/rv/r_workamp.htm - links to workamping sites

workersonwheels.com - job listings for Rvers

work-camping.com - Recreation Resource Management

camphost.org - provides staffing information for public recreation areas

happyvagabonds.com

kellyservices.com

koa.com/workatkoa – Kampgrounds of America

SUGGESTED READING

Support Your RV Lifestyle! An Insider's Guide to Working on the Road, by Jamie Hall (Pine Country Publishing, $19.95), presents very useful suggestions on how to make the RV lifestyle cost effective.

RV Retirement: How to Travel Part-Time or Full-Time In a Recreational Vehicle, by Jane Kenny (Roundabout Publications, $16.95), practical suggestions by an experienced RV traveler for more enriching RV lifestyle.

The Complete Idiot's Guide to RVing, Second Edition, by Brent Peterson, (Alpha Publishing, $18.95) contains up-to-date information on buying RVs, choosing campgrounds, and tips on where to go.

The Complete Book of Boondock RVing, Camping Off the Beaten Path, by Bill and Jan Moeller, (Ragged Mountain Press, $16.95) provides cost-effective information about dry camping along with all natural destinations.

Live Your Road Trip Dream: Travel for a Year for a Year for the Cost of Staying Home, by Phil White, (Rli Press, $18.95) offers inspiring adventures of a family that took to the road to explore.

RV Owner's Handbook, Revised, by Woodall Publications, $24.95 covers all aspects of RV ownership with an emphasis on maintenance.

Sightseein' and RVin': Travel Adventures After 50, by Sue and Ed Cook, (Trafford Publishing, $22.50) presents six years of adventures of an RV couple that traveled around the US, Mexico and Canada.

RV Living in the 21st Century: The Essential Reference Guide for All Rvers, by Peggi McDonald, (Authorhouse, $16.95) covers a large variety of topics related to the RV lifestyle.